40-DAY

Journey

WITH JOAN CHITTISTER

40-Day Journey Series

Beverly Lanzetta, Editor

Augsburg Books
Minneapolis

40-DAY JOURNEY WITH JOAN CHITTISTER

With two exceptions, scripture quotations under the heading *Biblical Wisdom* are taken from the *Holy Bible: New International Version*, published by Zondervan Publishing House, 1993. Scripture quotations for Journey Day 7, Sirach 7:32-35 and Journey Day 22, 3 John 1:5, 8 are taken from the *New Revised Standard Version Bible: Catholic Edition* © 1993 and 1989 by the Division of Christian Education of the National Council of Churches the National Council of the Churches of Christ in the USA. Used by permission. All rights reserved.

Cover design: Laurie Ingram
Cover photo: Bernadette Sullivan, OSB, of the Benedictine Sisters of Erie. Photo courtesy of Benetvision.

Library of Congress Cataloging-in-Publication Data
40-day journey with Joan Chittister / edited by Beverly Lanzetta.
    p. cm.
  ISBN 978-0-8066-8031-6 (alk. paper)
  1. Devotional exercises. 2. Chittister, Joan. I. Lanzetta, Beverly. II.
Title: Forty day journey with Joan Chittisler.
  BV4832.3.A15 2007
  242—dc22
          2007023098

The paper used in this publication meets the minimum requirements of American National Standard for Information Sciences—Permanence of Paper for Printed Library Materials, ANSI Z329.48-1984.

Printed in Canada.

11 10 09 08   4 5 6 7 8 9 10

CONTENTS

Series Introduction   7

Preface   9

How to Use this Book   11

Hints on Keeping a Journal   15

Who Is Joan Chittister?   17

Journey Day 1-40   22

Journey's End   103

For Further Reading   104

Notes   105

Sources   106

SERIES INTRODUCTION

Imagine spending forty days with a great spiritual guide who has both the wisdom and the experience to help you along the path of your own spiritual journey. Imagine being able to listen to and question spiritual guides from the past and the present. Imagine being, as it were, mentored by women and men who have made their own spiritual journey and have recorded the landmarks, detours, bumps in the road, potholes, and wayside rests that they encountered along the way—all to help others (like you) who must make their own journey.

The various volumes in Augsburg Books' *40-Day Journey Series* are all designed to do just that—to lead you where your mind and heart and spirit long to go. As Augustine once wrote: *"You have made us for yourself, O Lord, and our heart is restless until it rests in you."* The wisdom you will find in the pages of this series of books will give you the spiritual tools and direction to find that rest. But there is nothing quietistic in the spirituality you will find here. Those who would guide you on this journey have learned that the heart that rests in God is one that lives with deeper awareness, deeper creativity, deeper energy, and deeper passion and commitment to the things that matter to God.

An ancient Chinese proverb states the obvious: the journey of a thousand miles begins with the first step. In a deep sense, books in the *40-Day Journey Series* are first steps on a journey that will not end when the forty days are over. No one can take the first step (or any step) for you.

Imagine that you are on the banks of the Colorado River. You are here to go white-water rafting for the first time and your guide has just described the experience, telling you with graphic detail what to expect. It sounds both exciting and frightening. You long for the experience but are somewhat disturbed, anxious, uncertain in the face of the danger that promises to accompany you on the journey down the river. The guide gets into the raft. She will accompany you on the journey, *but she can't take the journey for you.* If you want to experience the wildness of the river, the raw beauty of the canyon, the camaraderie of adventurers, and the mystery of a certain oneness with nature (and nature's creator), then you've got to get in the boat.

This book in your hand is like that. It describes the journey, provides a "raft," and invites you to get in. Along with readings from your spiritual guide, you will find scripture to mediate on, questions to ponder, suggestions for personal journaling, guidance in prayer, and a prayer for the day. If done faithfully each day, you will find the wisdom and encouragement you need to integrate meaningful spiritual practices into your daily life. And when the 40-day journey is over it no longer will be the guide's description of the journey that stirs your longing for God but *your own experience* of the journey that grounds your faith and life and keeps you on the path.

I would encourage you to pick up other books in the series. There is only one destination, but many ways to get there. Not everything in every book will work for you (we are all unique), but in every book you will find much to help you discover your own path on the journey to the One in whom we all "live and move and have our being" (Acts 17:28)

May all be well with you on the journey.
Henry F. French, Series Editor

PREFACE

"To live is to venture beyond ourselves to taste the sweetness of the unknown." So says Sister Joan Chittister on the home page of her website, www.benetvision.org. The book in your hand is your invitation to experience the truth of it, your invitation *to live,* to venture beyond yourself into the mystery of the holy in the company of a woman of extraordinary spiritual depth.

To venture beyond yourself with Joan Chittister, however, is not to withdraw from the world; it is to engage the world deliberately on the side of life. As Sister Joan well knows, for those who would "taste the sweetness of the unknown," a risky and radical commitment to life—messy as it may be—is required.

In a *Meet the Press* interview with Tim Russert on Easter Sunday, 2006, Sister Joan made it clear that people of religious faith "must see life as our basic value." As you will discover in the pages that lie ahead, reverence for life and the Giver of life is the driving force behind Sister Joan's religious and political commitments; it is the passion behind her spiritual and moral engagement with the great and troubling issues of our time.

Joan Chittister's spirituality has been formed in the crucible of Benedictine monasticism. The spiritual disciplines of her tradition—prayer, work, religious reading and study, humility, community, and hospitality—have given Sister Joan a profound sense and understanding of the sacredness of the ordinary. She asks, "Why do people think the spiritual life demands withdrawal from the ordinary?" and in response she offers us a spirituality grounded in the realities of every day life, in the quotidian concerns of real people struggling for lives of real meaning and dignity.

To venture further into this book is to make a commitment of time; the time it will take to read, meditate, question, journal, and pray, and also the time it will take to begin living what you are learning. As Sister Joan once noted:

Time is sacred. Time is holy. Time is the raw material of the sacramental. Somehow or other we have to understand that this life is our life and the way we spend it is the kind of person we will, in the end, come to be.

Helping people become the kind of person they were created to be is Joan Chittister's compassionate desire.

It is not an easy journey, but it will be a rewarding one. As has been well said: "No one comes away from this woman without being spiritually and politically rearranged. Joan Chittister is a woman to be reckoned with."

In her book on the Psalms, *Songs of Joy*, Sister Joan noted that, "The Japanese say, 'One cannot learn to swim in a field.' If you want something to happen, the proverb implies, you have to go where it can… Wisdom is the fruit of reflection." This book is where spiritual transformation can happen. You will find much to reflect on and much wisdom for living from "a woman to be reckoned with" in the pages that lie ahead.

How to Use this Book

Your 40-day journey with Joan Chittister gives you the opportunity to be mentored by a great contemporary spiritual writer and Christian leader. The purpose of the journey, however, is not just to gain "head knowledge" about Joan Chittister. Rather, it is to begin living what you learn.

You will probably benefit most by fixing a special time of day in which to "meet with" your spiritual mentor. It is easier to maintain a spiritual practice if you do it regularly at the same time. For many people mornings, while the house is still quiet and before the busyness of the day begins, is a good time. Others will find that the noon hour or before bedtime serves well. We are all unique. Some of us are "morning people" and some of us are not. Do whatever works *for you* to maintain a regular meeting with Joan Chittister. Write it into your calendar and do your best to keep your appointments.

It is best if you complete your 40-day journey in forty days. A deepening focus and intensity of experience will be the result. However, it is certainly better to complete the journey than to give it up because you can't get it done in forty days. Indeed, making it a 40- or 20-week journey may better fit your schedule and it just might be that spending a whole week, or perhaps half a week, reflecting on the reading, the scripture, and the prayers, and then practicing what you are learning could be a powerfully transforming experience as well. Again, set a schedule that works for you, only be consistent.

Each day of the journey begins with a reading from Joan Chittister. You will note that the readings, from day to day, build on each other and introduce you to key ideas in her understanding of Christian life and faith. Read each selection slowly, letting the words sink into your consciousness. You may want to read each selection two or three times before moving on, perhaps reading it out loud once.

Following the reading from Chittister's writings, you will find the heading *Biblical Wisdom* and a brief passage from the Bible that relates directly to what she has said. As with the selection from Sister Joan, read the biblical text slowly, letting the words sink into your consciousness.

Following the biblical reading, you will find the heading *Silence for Meditation.* Here you should take anywhere from five to twenty minutes meditating on the two readings. Begin by getting centered. Sit with your back straight, eyes closed, hands folded in your lap, and breathe slowly and deeply. Remember that breath is a gift of God, it is God's gift of life. Do nothing for two or three minutes other than simply observe your breath. Focus your awareness on the end of your nose. Feel the breath enter through your nostrils and leave through your nostrils.

Once you feel your mind and spirit settling down, open your eyes and read the reading and the biblical text again. Read them slowly, focus on each word or phrase, savor them, explore possible meanings and implications. At the end of each day you will find a blank space with the heading *Notes.* As you meditate on the readings, jot down any insights that occur to you. Do the readings raise any questions for you? Write them down. Do the readings suggest anything you should do? Write it down.

Stay at it as long as it feels useful. When your mind is ready to move on, close your eyes and observe your breath for a minute or so. Then return to the book and the next heading: *Questions to Ponder.* Here you will find a few pointed questions by Beverly Lanzetta, the book's compiler and editor, on the day's reading. These are general questions intended for all spiritual seekers and communities of faith. Think them through and write your answers (and the implications of your answers for your own life of faith and for your community of faith) in the *Notes* section.

Many of these *Questions to Ponder* are designed to remind us that, although spirituality is always personal, it is simultaneously relational and communal. A number of the questions, therefore, apply the relevance of the day's reading to faith communities. Just remember, a faith community may be as large as a regular organized gathering of any religious tradition or as small as a family or the relationship between spiritual friends. You don't need to be a member of a church, synagogue, mosque, or temple to be part of a faith community. Answer the questions in the context of your particular faith community.

Then move on to the heading *Psalm Fragments.* Here you will find a brief verse or two from the Hebrew book of Psalms that relate to the day's reading. The Psalms have always been the mainstay of monastic prayer in the Christian tradition and thus a mainstay of Joan Chittister's life as a Benedictine sister.

Reflect for a moment on the *Psalm Fragment* and then continue on to the heading *Journal Reflections.* Several suggestions for journaling are given that apply the readings to your own personal experience. It is in journaling that the "day" reaches its climax and the potential for transformative change is greatest. It would be best to buy a separate journal rather than use the *Notes* section of the book. For a journal you can use a spiral-bound or ring-bound notebook or one of the hardcover journal books sold in stationery stores. Below are some suggestions for how to keep a journal. For now, let's go back to the 40-day journey book.

The *Questions to Ponder* and *Journal Reflection* exercises are meant to assist you in reflecting on the daily reading and scripture quotations. Do not feel that you have to answer every question. You may choose which questions or exercises are most helpful to you. Sometimes a perfectly appropriate response to a question is, "I don't know" or "I'm not sure what I think about that." The important thing is to record your own thoughts and questions.

After *Journal Reflections*, you will find two more headings. The first is *Prayers of Hope & Healing*. As a member of a religious community, Joan Chittister knows well that one of the highest services a Christian can perform is prayer for family and friends, for one's community of faith, for the victims of injustice, and for one's enemies. Under this heading you will find suggestions for prayer that relate to the key points in the day's readings. The last heading (before *Notes*) is *Prayer for Today*, a one or two line prayer to end your "appointment" with Joan Chittister, and to be prayed from time to time throughout the day.

Hints on Keeping a Journal

A journal is a very helpful tool. Keeping a journal is a form of meditation, a profound way of getting to know yourself—and God—more deeply. Although you could read your 40-day journey book and reflect on it "in your head," writing can help you focus your thoughts, clarify your thinking, and keep a record of your insights, questions, and prayers. Writing is generative: it enables you to have thoughts you would not otherwise have had.

A few hints for journaling

1. Write in your journal with grace. Don't get stuck in trying to do it perfectly. Just write freely. Don't worry about literary style, spelling, or grammar. Your goal is simply to generate thoughts pertinent to your own life and get them down on paper.
2. You may want to begin and end your journaling with prayer. Ask for the guidance and wisdom of the Spirit (and thank God for that guidance and wisdom when you are done).
3. If your journaling takes you in directions that go beyond the journaling questions in your 40-day book, go there. Let the questions encourage, not limit, your writing.
4. Respond honestly. Don't write what you think you're supposed to believe. Write down what you really do believe, in so far as you can identify that. If you don't know, or are not sure, or if you have questions, record those. Questions are often openings to spiritual growth.
5. Carry your 40-day book and journal around with you every day during your journey (only keep them safe from prying eyes). The 40-day journey process is an intense experience that doesn't stop when you close the book. Your mind and heart and spirit will be engaged all day, and it will be helpful to have your book and journal handy to take notes or make new entries as they occur to you.

Journeying with Others

You can use your 40-day book with another person, a spiritual friend, or partner, or with a small group. It would be best for each person first do his or her own reading, reflection, and writing in solitude. Then when you come together, share the insights you have gained from your time alone. Your discussion will probably focus on the *Questions to Ponder*; however, if the relationship is intimate, you may feel comfortable sharing some of what you have written in your journal. No one, however, should ever be pressured to share anything in their journal if they are not comfortable doing so.

Remember that your goal is to learn from one another, not to argue, nor to prove that you are right and the other person wrong. Just practice listening and trying to understand why your partner, friend, or colleague thinks as he or she does.

Practicing intercessory prayer together, you will find, strengthens the spiritual bonds of those who take the journey together. And as you all work to translate insight into action, sharing your experience with each other is a way of encouraging and guiding each other and provides the opportunity to correct each other gently if that becomes necessary.

Continuing the Journey

When the forty days (or forty weeks) are over, a milestone has been reached, but the journey needn't end. One goal of the 40-day series is to introduce you to a particular spiritual guide with the hope that, having whet your appetite, you will want to keep the journey going. At the end of the book are some suggestions for further reading that will take you deeper on your journey with your mentor.

WHO IS JOAN CHITTISTER?

For over twenty-five years, Joan Chittister has been a passionate voice for the spiritual renewal of our planet. An international figure, she has been recognized by universities and organizations around the world for her work in peace, justice, spirituality, interreligious dialogue, and the equality of women in church and society.

A Benedictine sister and former prioress of the Benedictine sisters of Erie, Pennsylvania, Sister Joan is a regular columnist for the National Catholic Reporter, past president of the Leadership Conference of Women Religious, founding member of the International Committee for the Peace Council, co-chair of the Global Peace Initiative of Women Religious and Spiritual Leaders, and founder and director of Benetvision (www.benetvision.org), a resource and research center for contemporary spirituality. Most recently, she has co-founded the Network of Spiritual Progressives, a new national movement focused on the integration of contemplation and activism. In all of these efforts, her most enduring legacy is her commitment to peace and justice, and her capacity to bring relevant spiritual questions to contemporary life.

Born April 26, 1936, Sister Joan experienced loss at the age of three when her father died. Her first attraction to religious life occurred at his funeral when she became captivated by three monastic women praying over her father's coffin. It was in these formative years, when her Irish-Catholic mother married Harold (Dutch) Chittister, a Presbyterian, that the foundation for Joan Chittister's future theology was laid.

Raised as a Catholic, her life-long concern for religious openness and interreligious dialogue was firmly established in the second grade when a teaching sister informed her class that only Catholics went to heaven. Joan was stunned by this assertion as her father and all of her Chittister relatives were Protestants. In the passion of youth and the heat of thought, she rushed home to question her mother about the truth or falsity of this statement.

Questioning became a central theme in the ensuing years as the tension of seemingly contradictory beliefs and lifestyles occupied her thought. At the age of sixteen, Joan entered Mount St. Benedict's Monastery in Erie, Pennsylvania. Her resilient spirit was honed when, just weeks later, she came down with polio and ended up in a wheelchair and iron lung. Her tenacity in overcoming polio fortified her for future life disappointments, setbacks, and loss of faith.

During her early years in the monastery, she cared deeply about two things—religious life and writing. Yet the seemingly insurmountable conflict between them took years of soul searching to resolve. A committed monastic, she nevertheless rejected any narrow interpretation of the church's teachings. In her heart she knew that the spirit of love could not be subsumed by or made the fodder of theological or social bias. A lover of writing, she wondered how she could reconcile her passion for language with her equally strong bond to religious life. The tension between these two commitments, and her struggle to reconcile their limitations and gifts, forged her prophetic writing voice.

A prolific author, she has published more than thirty books. The titles tell us something about her deepest commitments: *Wisdom Distilled from the Daily*; *Scarred by Struggle, Transformed by Hope*; *Becoming Fully Human*; *The Friendship of Women*; *Illuminated Life*; *In Search of Belief*. While the emphasis in these books is on spiritual issues, her spirituality is not a shy, conventional affair. To the contrary, her voice is born of a passion for truth and a bold quest for justice and peace. Nor is there anything parochial or narrow in her thought. Nothing that affects planetary harmony or ameliorates suffering escapes her notice or her pen. Her interests are far-reaching and her vision broad and deep, as she confronts church policies, governmental politics, religious violence, ordination of women, poverty, racism, and the rights of gays and minority groups everywhere.

Sister Joan is a guide through what she calls a "crossover moment" in history—where the big questions all demand new answers, and we are caught between letting go of prior truths and striving forward to new truths not yet formed. Fully open to the present moment, Sister Joan leads pilgrims on an exodus from the bondage of consumerism and social apathy to the freedom of inner wisdom and spiritual integrity.

What makes her writing so accessible to the reader is her earthy and practical approach to spiritual life and her personal openness. Most of her books are sprinkled with stories of her struggles and hopes, loneliness and community, pain and deep gratitude for life. With an eye toward the needs of a thirsting world, she tackles concerns that affect all humans, and cries out with a bold and impassioned voice against injustice, ignorance, and war.

Underneath it all rests Sister Joan's personal experience of excessive hope and radical grace. In her life encounter with disappointment, lost opportunities, and soul wounds, she mines a spirituality that reaches into the souls of others because they recognize that she, too, has been there. She reminds us that the Spirit's movement is mysterious and we never know how or in what way we will be irrevocably changed.

She has been a Benedictine sister now for almost fifty-five years. In the ancient rule of Benedict, she finds a lifestyle that has endured the test of time and a spirituality that affirms her fullness of being. Stabilized by a community of women monastics, Sister Joan has been able to reach out to the troubled, pained, hopeless, and dying around the world. Rooted in the Benedictine spirituality of hospitality, Sister Joan has expanded this ancient wisdom to devote her life to the reversal of injustice and the resurrection of hope. She has been called a prophet of our times, a voice for the voiceless, and a woman in search of truth. Her commitment to contemplation in action is testimony to the loving presence of God in creation.

This *40-Day Journey with Joan Chittister* is designed to be a contemplative resource for daily study and practice. In selecting the daily readings, I have had the privilege of reading through many of Joan Chittister's writings and books. I have chosen passages that reflect her wide range of concerns and the spiritual significance of her thought. To assist in your daily contemplative practice, I include Biblical quotes and reflection questions that enlarge on the chosen spiritual passage. Each of the forty days of reflection concludes with an original prayer I wrote as part of my own meditation on her writings. It is my hope that you will find as much solace, insight, and fire in your *40-Day Journey with Joan Chittister* as I have found in the editorial process.

Beverly Lanzetta

40-Day

Journey

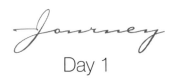

Day 1

SPIRITUALITY IS ABOUT THE HUNGER in the human heart. It seeks not only a way to exist, but a reason to exist that is beyond the biological or the institutional or even the traditional. It lifts religion up from the level of the theoretical or the mechanical to the personal. It seeks to make real the things of the spirit. It transcends rules and rituals to a concentration on meaning. It pursues in depth the mystical dimensions of life that religion purports to promote.

When we develop a spiritual life that is beyond some kind of simple, unthinking attachment to an inherited canon of behaviors, the soul goes beyond adherence to a system to the growth of the soul. Spirituality seeks to transcend the functionaries of religion to achieve an intimacy of its own with the mystery of the universe. Spirituality takes religion into its own hands.

᛫

BIBLICAL WISDOM

Since we live by the Spirit, let us keep in step with the Spirit. Galatians 5:25

SILENCE FOR MEDITATION

QUESTIONS TO PONDER

- What are alternatives to spirituality that our culture promotes as ways to satisfy the "hunger of the human heart"? Do they work?
- If spirituality "transcends rules and rituals," what do we do with all the rules and rituals of religious life? Do they still matter?
- How might worship change if its goal was the experience of intimacy "with the mystery of the universe" rather than belief in creeds and doctrines?

Psalm Fragments

I stretch out my hands to you;
my soul thirsts for you like a parched land. Psalm 143:6

Journal Reflections

- In what way is your spiritual hunger nourished? Write about what nourishes you spiritually and what depletes you.
- Meditate on how spirituality seeks to "transcend the functionaries of religion" to bring you into greater intimacy with God. How does that happen?
- Journal about how, in your own life, a spiritual commitment "[took] religion into its own hands."

Prayers of Hope & Healing

Pray for your community of faith that it might be a place where intimacy with the mystery of the universe is affirmed and where people are encouraged to "pursue the mystical dimensions of life." Pray for your spiritual friends that you may be mutually supportive of each other as you tend to "the growth of the soul."

Prayer for Today

May I grow closer to you with each day, my dearest God. May you fill my spiritual hunger with your overflowing love.

Notes

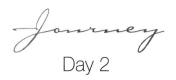

Day 2

EVERY MAJOR RELIGIOUS TRADITION SPEAKS of some kind of enlightenment. To the Christian, it is union with God; to the Hindu, nirvana or freedom from all things; to the Buddhist, desirelessness; to the Muslim, submission to the will of God. In all of them, in other words, lies the consciousness that there is in us a tension between two opposing poles. At one level we seek only the gratification of the self for its own sake. At that stage we struggle against every period of life. At the other level, we achieve the transcendence of the self to the point where no external changes can disturb the balance of what we call the soul.

Enlightenment is not the characteristic of one kind of person only, the ancients teach… No one is more disposed than another to reach enlightenment, in other words. We can each achieve enlightenment, we can each come to wisdom, but only by virtue of the choice we make from moment to moment, from situation to situation.

͐

BIBLICAL WISDOM

The true light that enlightens every man was coming into the world. . . . [T]o all who received him, to those who believed in his name, he gave the right to become children of God. John 1:9, 12

SILENCE FOR MEDITATION

QUESTIONS TO PONDER

- In what ways does our culture encourage or discourage, contribute to or diminish the quest for enlightenment?
- Do you believe that "no one is more disposed than another to reach enlightenment"? How does this belief affect your own spiritual life and the life together of your faith community?
- Should "transcendence of the self" be actively promoted by religious communities? Why or why not? What would have to change if this were to happen?

Psalm Fragments

My mouth shall speak wisdom;
the meditation of my heart shall be understanding. Psalm 49:3

Journal Reflections

- Meditate on whether you feel called to deeper self-realization. What does enlightenment mean to you?
- In what way does your own desire for union with God take you beyond "seeking gratification of the self"?
- Meditate on *your* reason to exist. How is your reason to exist reflected in your personal and professional relationships?

Prayers of Hope & Healing

Pray for your family, that they grow with you "moment by moment" toward greater communion and honesty. Pray for loved ones who are dying, that the Spirit will gently guide them toward transcendence of self. Pray for your spiritual friends that the Divine will draw them to the point where nothing "can disturb the balance of what we call the soul."

Prayer for Today

Free me, Holy One, from seeking my own gratification, and conform my whole being to your loving embrace.

Notes

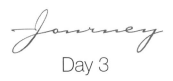

Day 3

THE VERY PURPOSE OF RELIGION is to enable us to step off into the uncharted emptiness that is the spiritual life, freely but not untethered. We have under our feet the promise of the tradition that formed us and the disciplines that shaped our souls. We can then wander through the pantheon of spiritual traditions freely, going deeper and deeper into every question from every direction. In the end, then, we become more, not less, of what we ourselves know to be our own religious identity.

It isn't so much that people leave religion, I think, as it is that, like Olympic runners on a mission, they come to a moment in life when they go beyond the system to the very source of the light. It is the plight of the mystic to enter the universe of God alone where no charts or maps or signs exist to guide us and assure us of the way. It is a serious and disturbing moment, one after which we are never quite the same.

BIBLICAL WISDOM

Then will the lame leap like a deer, and the mute tongue shout for joy. Water will gush forth in the wilderness and streams in the desert. Isaiah 35:6

SILENCE FOR MEDITATION

QUESTIONS TO PONDER

- Does your community of faith encourage its members to "step off into the uncharted emptiness" of the spiritual life? If so, how? If not, why not?
- If the purpose of the spiritual life is to take us beyond religion "to the very source of the light," then what benefits does religion offer to the spiritually-minded person?
- How would religion need to change in order to prepare its members to enter the moment of aloneness, that point of discovery where there are "no charts or maps or signs"?

Psalm Fragments

Let me hear of your steadfast love in the morning,
* for in you I put my trust.*
* Teach me the way I should go,*
* for to you I lift up my soul.* Psalm 143:8

Journal Reflections

- How has your relationship to religion changed over the years? Do you feel called beyond formal religion to "the very source of light"? If so, how have you experienced that call?
- Reflect on how your religious tradition positively formed you. What spiritual disciplines have shaped your soul?
- Meditate on what Joan Chittister calls "the plight of the mystic." Have you been touched by this mystical call? If so, write about the experience.

Prayers of Hope & Healing

Offer a prayer for your spiritual community that all may love each other in an unbounded way. Pray for your religious tradition that it will be opened to the beauty of differences and the capacity to grow in the light. Pray that our world will embrace the true heart of religion and ameliorate the suffering of creation.

Prayer for Today

May you lead me, God, beyond all definitions and restrictions into your heart of hearts, where the light of divine love is All.

Notes

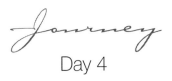

Day 4

THE BENEDICTINE SPIRITUALITY OF COMMUNITY is based on life with other persons in the spirit of Christ: to support them, to empower them, and to learn from them. The radical monastic testimony of this commitment to universal human love is celibacy, the public declaration that the monastic will belong to everyone and to no one at the same time. Celibacy says that human community is built on a great deal more than the sexual, that it transcends sexual love, and pours itself out with no expectation of outpouring in return. Community, the Rule reminds us, is to be built on "chaste" love, on love that does not use or exploit the other, on love that can give without requiring equal payment in return, on love that is not based on the gratification of the self. And that is exactly why the Benedictine spirituality of community is not for celibates alone.

In a culture in which sex has become a consuming issue, a national passion, an underlying current in every social stream, Benedictine spirituality calls for love in breadth and love in depth and love in human, rather than in simply sexual, terms. The spirituality of celibacy says that each of us is whole before God, that God has absolute priority for us, that God is sufficient for us, and that God's demands over our lives are total. The married, the single, and the monastic all have this same call to ultimate aloneness and ultimate union with God, and eventually every life will bow to it.

૮

BIBLICAL WISDOM

And we, who with unveiled faces all reflect the Lord's glory, are being transformed into his likeness with ever-increasing glory. 2 Corinthians 3:18

SILENCE FOR MEDITATION

Questions to Ponder

- In what way might the celibate life be spiritually beneficial today? What kinds of personal challenges might be encountered when considering this option?
- Monastic traditions emphasize and value the celibate over the married life. Is this a realistic distinction for people today? Why or why not?
- How might "chaste love" be experienced in the married or partnered life?

Psalm Fragments

Steadfast love and faithfulness will meet;
righteousness and peace will kiss each other. Psalm 85:10

Journal Reflections

- Contemplate the celibate life. Have you ever felt drawn to the celibate life? If so, why? If not, reflect on why someone might feel drawn to celibacy.
- How would you draw the distinction between "love in human, rather than in simply sexual, terms"?
- If you affirmed "ultimate aloneness and ultimate union with God" as central to your life, how might it change your relationships? Meditate on whether or not God might be leading you in this direction?

Prayers of Hope & Healing

Pray to understand the spirit of love and how sexuality and deep love are the fruit of "ultimate aloneness with God." Pray for your family, partners, and colleagues that they each might become "whole before God," and know the beauty of "chaste love."

Prayer for Today

I long to be alone with you, my Beloved. Please teach me the wisdom of spiritual celibacy.

Notes

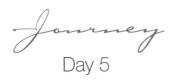

Day 5

CONTEMPLATIVES ARE PEOPLE WHOSE CONSCIOUSNESS of God permeates their entire lives. Their awareness of God's presence magnetizes them and directs them beyond everything else, beyond all other values. Contemplatives are aware that God creates them, sustains them, and challenges them. As a result, all other values and agendas fall away. I don't mean contemplatives find no value in other things—for example, in a career, or money, or achievement. These things, however, never become their greatest value. The awareness of God's presence remains the greatest value.

In essence, according to all the great mystics, contemplation is, and I think continues to be, this consciousness of living steeped in God, of being surrounded by God, of being directed by God, of being in the presence of God, of learning to see life through the eyes of God, of being aware of God's love, action, and challenge.

ᶜ

BIBLICAL WISDOM

As the deer longs for streams of water, so my soul thirsts for you, O God! Psalms 42:1

SILENCE FOR MEDITATION

QUESTIONS TO PONDER

- Do you believe that contemplative prayer and a contemplative lifestyle are important to contemporary spiritual life? Why or why not?
- What limits or obstacles does society place on the quest for holiness?
- There seem to be many faith communities that do little to encourage the experience of "living steeped in God." Why do you think that is so?

Psalm Fragments

Be still, and know that I am God! Psalm 46:10

Journal Reflections

- Do you allow money, career, or achievement to become the greatest values in your life? If so, how might you overcome these attractions?
- Write about some situation or relationship that reminds you of God's presence at the center of your life.
- Meditate on your awareness of "God's love, action, and challenge" in the world around you.

Prayers of Hope & Healing

Pray for family, friends, and colleagues that they will be drawn ever closer to their spiritual desire, and that God will be present to them in times of suffering and in times of joy. Allow God's loving embrace to fill you and your loved ones with a renewed sense of grace.

Prayer for Today

May I be given the wisdom to be centered in my heart, O God, until my whole life is the measure of your love.

Notes

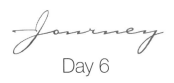
Day 6

WHEN POETS TALK ABOUT THE human soul, they do not talk about reason; they talk about feeling. The totally human human being, they enable us to see, is the one who weeps over evil, revels in goodness, loves outrageously, and carries the pain of the world in healing hands. Feeling is the mark of saints. . . Feeling, we know deep within us, signifies the real measure of a soul.

Without feeling, living becomes one long bland journey to nowhere that tastes of nothing. Take feeling away, and we take away life. Feeling warns of our excesses, and alerts us to possibilities. It attaches us and opens us and warns us of danger. Because of our feelings we are able to persevere through hard times and find our way to good times. Feelings lead us to the people who love us through life and satisfy our souls when nothing else about a situation can sustain us at all. Feelings, devoid of thought, made only of mist, become the inner lights that lead us out of harm's way and home to our better selves. Feeling leads us to love the God we cannot see and to see the God around whom we have yet to come to love.

BIBLICAL WISDOM

Place me like a seal over your heart, like a seal on your arm; for love is as strong as death, . . . It burns like blazing fire, like a mighty flame. Many waters cannot quench love; rivers cannot wash it away. Song of Solomon 8:6-7

SILENCE FOR MEDITATION

QUESTIONS TO PONDER

- Does your faith community encourage or discourage openness to and expression of feelings? Why?
- Do you agree that the "totally human being" must learn to feel deeply and experience deeply in order to live spiritually? Why or why not?

- Have you experienced your community of faith as a place that "weeps over evil, revels in goodness, loves outrageously, and carries the pain of the world in healing hands"? How might religious communities more faithfully live up to this vision?

Psalm Fragments

I will sing and make melody.
Awake, my soul!
Awake, O harp and lyre!
I will awake the dawn. Psalm 57:7b-8

Journal Reflections

- Meditate on how your deepest feelings have helped you grow in your spiritual life.
- Write about some time when you have ignored your deepest feelings. What were the consequences?
- In what ways are your feelings suppressed? In which situations are your feelings given expression? Journal about the difference and its implication for your spiritual life.

Prayers of Hope & Healing

Pray that your heart will open wide to the suffering of others. Pray for our communities and nations to be more gentle and tender in their treatment of human and planetary ills. Pray for healing of the wound of not-feeling for you, your family, and spiritual friends.

Prayer for Today

O, God, you love me with your whole being. Please heal my wounded heart and allow me to feel the depth of your desire.

Notes

Journey

Day 7

[THOMAS] MERTON'S MONASTICISM WAS A revolution equaled only by the origin of Benedictine monasticism itself. Until the sixth century, monasticism had been an exercise in private and personal spirituality. It was Benedict who, in the sixth century, made human community itself the essence of sanctity. Merton's monasticism, too, was a revolution that took monasticism out of the confines of the local monastery and situated it in a concern for world community itself. Merton's monasticism was a monasticism concentrated on the presence of God in the present.

Merton saw the world through a heart uncluttered by formulas and undimmed by systems. He taught more than piety and asceticism for its own sake. He taught concepts that flew in the face of tradition then and fly in the face of culture still: the sin of poverty, the moral imperative of peace, the rectitude of stewardship, the holy power of nonviolence, the sanctity of globalism, and the essence of enlightenment. Merton sowed seeds of contemplation that led to action, an often forgotten but always bedrock spiritual concept.

BIBLICAL WISDOM

Stretch out your hand to the poor, so that your blessing may be complete. Do not avoid those who weep, but mourn with those who mourn. Do not hesitate to visit the sick, because for such deeds you will be loved. Sirach 7:32-35

SILENCE FOR MEDITATION

QUESTIONS TO PONDER

- In what sense is "human community itself the essence of sanctity"?
- How might a *monastic mindset* on the part of ordinary Christians change their concern for "world community"?
- Why did Merton (and Joan Chittister) link contemplation and action?

Psalm Fragments

I know that the LORD maintains the cause of the needy,
* and executes justice for the poor.*
Surely the righteous shall give thanks to your name;
the upright shall live in your presence. Psalm 143:12-13

Journal Reflections

- Review your commitments to alleviating poverty and promoting peace and nonviolence. Do you feel called to do more?
- Write about the ways in which your spiritual life reflects the universal values Merton espoused. Reflect on how your spiritual practice might contribute to the diminishment of suffering in everyday life.
- What impedes—and what helps—your ability to adopt a *monastic mindset*?

Prayers of Hope & Healing

Pray for the renewal of contemplative wisdom in you, your family, and community. Pray for the strength to lead a life of spiritual commitment and joyful solitude so your soul will grow in contemplation of God.

Prayer for Today

May I feel, O God, the passion of your love for those who suffer and are downtrodden by the sins of the world.

Notes

Day 8

GRATITUDE IS NOT A REACTION; it is a state of mind. When we go through life cultivating the ability to be grateful that it's not raining, that we are not sick, that we have good friends if not a lot of resources, and that we have found things we like to do, we are rich enough inside to sustain whatever we might lose around us.

To be grateful and to be thankful are not the same thing. It's easy to be polite and not mean it. It's spiritual to be grateful, to do to another what has been done for us. "Thankfulness," Henri Amiel wrote, "may consist merely of words. Gratitude is shown in acts." To nourish a spirit of gratitude requires us to repay in kind what has been done for us.

↵

BIBLICAL WISDOM

Let the word of Christ dwell in you richly as you teach and admonish one another with all wisdom, and as you sing psalms, hymns, and spiritual songs with gratitude in your hearts to God. Colossians 3:16

SILENCE FOR MEDITATION

QUESTIONS TO PONDER

- How are being "grateful" and being "thankful" different? Do you agree that gratitude is more spiritual? Why or why not?
- How would cultivating gratitude as "a state of mind" be beneficial both personally and socially? What specific practices would assist in cultivating gratitude?
- How does God fit in with the idea that being grateful "requires us to repay in kind what has been done for us"?

Psalm Fragments

I trust in the steadfast love of God
  forever and ever.
I will thank you forever,
  because of what you have done. Psalm 52:8a-9b

Journal Reflections

- Reflect on the ways you feel and express gratitude for your life.
- What would help you in your present relationships to further cultivate gratitude as a deepening state of consciousness?
- List all the gifts you receive each day. Reflect on the many "givers" in your life. How can you remain mindful of the preciousness and giftedness of life?

Prayers of Hope & Healing

Pray that a deep well of gratitude will overflow your soul and fill your heart with love. Pray for the healing of human arrogance, disrespect, and greed. Envision all of creation embraced in the light of generosity and wisdom.

Prayer for Today

Humble me, my God, until my heart overflows with gratitude for all the blessings you bestow on me this day.

Notes

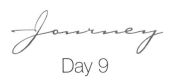

Day 9

AN ESTIMATED 450 MILLION WOMEN in developing countries live crippled, stunted lives due to childhood protein-energy malnutrition that comes from feeding girls the leftovers of men's meals. They are married young, sold young, passed from man to man young, put to work young, and die young—if they are allowed to live at all. What Third World mother wants to bring a girl-child into the world to suffer as she has, to be rejected as she has been rejected, to be deprived of her own young life in order to breed other young lives, as she has been deprived? It is a storm of sorrow, a deluge of pain that describes the lives of the women of the world.

It starts when they are infants and it follows them to their graves. Not all women find themselves in abusive situations certainly. Those are the lucky ones, of course. But they are given, nevertheless. They do not lead autonomous lives. They do not make decisions about schools or careers. They do not dream dreams and develop ideas. They do not travel around the world. They do not travel to the next village. They do not leave the house. They do not leave the harem. They were born to be used, abused, and abandoned when no longer useful. And no one asks them what they want or what they think, ever.

༄

BIBLICAL WISDOM

Does not wisdom call, and does not understanding raise her voice? On the heights, beside the way, at the crossroads she takes her stand; beside the gates in front of the town, at the entrance of the portals she cries out. Proverbs 8:1-3

SILENCE FOR MEDITATION

Questions to Ponder

- What political or social causes and cultural norms contribute to the suffering of women in developing countries?
- Are there both subtle and not-so-subtle expressions of these conditions in this country? How are they fostered and bred?
- What happens to the spirit of women who are *owned* and abused? How does this affect the well-being of all life? What does it do to the feminine in creation?

Psalm Fragments

Young men and women alike,
    old and young together! Psalm 148:12

Journal Reflections

- Meditate on the lives of women around the world who live in poverty and under social oppression. Write about your feelings.
- Do the many ways of violence against women affected your spiritual life? How? Or why not?
- Reflect in your journal on how you have experienced (as a woman or a man) violence against girls and women.

Prayers of Hope & Healing

Pray for women around the world who are suffering today, who have no food, or are deprived of basic life necessities. Pray for women and men everywhere that the spirit of the women and the strength of the feminine will fill their hearts. Pray for the healing of violence in the hearts of humanity.

Prayer for Today

O, Divine Mother, may my heart be opened to the suffering of women and girls, and may our institutions be capable of healing the violence against our beloved sisters everywhere.

Notes

Day 10

TIME PRESSES UPON US AND tells us we're too busy to be contemplative, but our souls know better. Souls die from lack of reflection. Responsibilities dog us and tell us we're too involved with the "real" world to be concerned about the spiritual question. But it is always spiritual questions that make a difference in the way we go about our public responsibilities. Marriage, business, children, professions are all defined to keep contemplation out. We go about them as if there were no inherent spiritual dimension to them when the fact of the matter is that no one needs contemplation more than the harried mother, the irritable father, the ambitious executive, the striving professional, the poor woman, the sick man. . . Where can we go for a model of another way to live when we have no choice but to live the way we do?

The desert monastics, alone in the wilderness of fourth-century Egypt, wrestled with the elements of life, plumbed its basics, tested its truths, and passed on their wisdom to those who sought it out. . . Abba Sisoes said, "Seek God, and not where God lives." We live and breathe, grow and develop in the womb of God. And yet we seek God elsewhere—in defined places, in special ways, on mountaintops and in caves, on specific days and with special ceremonies. But the life that is full of light knows that God is not over there; God is here. And for the taking. The question is only how.

ᕫ

BIBLICAL WISDOM

Do not be afraid . . . Since the first day that you set your mind to gain understanding and to humble yourself before your God, your words were heard, and I have come in response to them. Daniel 10:12

SILENCE FOR MEDITATION

Questions to Ponder

- What might happen if communities of faith actively encouraged their members to "seek God, and not where God lives"?
- What cultural and religious forces and beliefs prevent the deeper spiritual life from taking root in daily life?
- How might family and professional relations change if their "inherent spiritual dimension" were acknowledged and acted upon?

Psalm Fragments

Glory in his holy name;
let the hearts of those who seek the LORD rejoice.
Seek the LORD and his strength;
seek his presence continually. Psalm 105:3-4

Journal Reflections

- Meditate on the influences in your life that distract or impede your desire to be more contemplative.
- Would you say that your life "is full of light"? If yes, describe the experience and its impact on you and others. If no, does it seem possible for you? Why or why not?
- Explore in your journal ways in which you might develop contemplative focus and spiritual determination.

Prayers of Hope & Healing

Pray for your family, community, and colleagues that the Spirit will enliven them and give them the strength to seek God in all things. Pray for the courage to enter the "womb of God" and find there your own solitude. May the spiritual dimension of life heal the fragmentation of our hearts.

Prayer for Today

Show me, Holy One, how I may draw closer to you in daily life. Give me the courage to seek you alone in all I do and all I am.

Notes

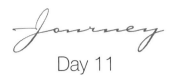

Day 11

ONE OF THE MOST DIFFICULT, but seasoning, elements of life is simply the fine art of getting up every morning, of doing what must be done if for no other reason than that it is our responsibility to do it. To face the elements of the day and keep on going takes a peculiar kind of courage. It is in dailiness that we prove our mettle. And it is not easy.

The easy thing to do is run away from life. Anyone can do it, and everyone at one time or another wants to. Living through the sterile and fruitless cycles of life earns no medals, carries no honor... Few, in the end, ever go, of course. But simply staying where we are because there is nowhere else to go is not the answer. What makes the difference is to stay where we need to be with a sense that dailiness is the real stuff of contemplation. Then the staying becomes more than bearable; it becomes possible.

BIBLICAL WISDOM

The time is surely coming, says the Lord, when the one who plows shall overtake the one who reaps, and the treader of grapes the one who sows the seeds; the mountains shall drip sweet wine, and all the hills shall flow with it. Amos 9:13

SILENCE FOR MEDITATION

QUESTIONS TO PONDER

- Do you agree that "in dailiness we prove our mettle"? Why or why not?
- What is needed to foster awareness that everyday events—getting up in the morning, going to work, caring for loved ones—are the medium through which God is present to us?
- In what sense is dailiness the "real stuff of contemplation"?

Psalm Fragments

You cause the grass to grow for the cattle,
  and plants for people to use,
  to bring forth food from the earth,
  and wine to gladden the human heart,
  oil to make the face shine,
  and bread to strengthen the human heart. Psalm 104:14-15

Journal Reflections

- Make a list of your daily responsibilities and commitments. What do you think about them? Do they feel like the "real stuff of contemplation" to you? Why or why not?
- Do you ever "run away from life"? If so, what makes you do that? What would be different if you ran to life instead of from life?
- Where do you "need to be"? Is it possible to go there and stay there with joy? What would it take?

Prayers of Hope & Healing

Pray for all those this day who labor to provide for loved ones, that God will grant them serenity and peace. Pray for insight, so you may see and feel honestly your own heart and its longings. May the daily round of events in your life become the seeds of new contemplation.

Prayer for Today

May I have the determination and the faith to continue to seek you, God, in the trials and joys of every day.

Notes

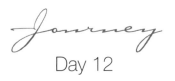

Day 12

THE CONTEMPLATIVE IS THE ONE among us in whom prayer, deep reflection on the presence and activity of God in the self and the world, has come little by little to extinguish the illusion of autonomy and the enthronement of the self that make little kingdoms of us all. The contemplative goes beyond the self, and all its delusions, to Life itself. One prayer at a time, contemplatives allow the heart of God to beat in the heart they call their own.

The contemplative is the seeker who can go down into the self, down the tunnel of emptiness, and, finding nothing but God in the center of life, call that Everything. Most of all, the contemplative is the one who, looking at the world, sees nothing but the presence and activity of God everywhere, in everyone. How can this be possible? Because to be a contemplative, prayer is the key to the dialogue and, eventually, to the Silence that is Everything.

BIBLICAL WISDOM

This is what the Lord says to me: "I will remain quiet and will look on from my dwelling place, like shimmering heat in the sunshine, like a cloud of dew in the heat of harvest." Isaiah 18:4

SILENCE FOR MEDITATION

QUESTIONS TO PONDER

- In what, if any, positive ways does your community of faith help "to extinguish the illusion of autonomy and the enthronement of the self"?
- Do you agree or disagree that it is "the contemplative" who is able to "go down into the self, down the tunnel of emptiness"? If so, how?
- In what way does culture contribute to the "enthronement of the self"? In such a culture, how can people become more "empty," more selfless, and thus more open to God at the center of being?

Psalm Fragments

Let my prayer be counted as incense before you,
and the lifting up of my hands as an evening sacrifice. Psalm 141:2

Journal Reflections

- Meditate on whether you feel called to silence.
- Are you weary of the needs and delusions of the self? If so, what can you do about it? If not, do you think *self-emptying* is a good or bad idea? Why?
- Meditate on what, if any, ways you experience "the heart of God to beat" in your own heart? Describe the experience or the longing for the experience.

Prayers of Hope & Healing

Pray for your family and spiritual community that they will be led away from the false self to the "center of life," where God is "Everything." Pray for our national and world leaders that peace and compassion will guide their actions, rather than the delusion of autonomy. Pray for the healing of self-motivated actions that wound and destroy community.

Prayer for Today

O Lord, make me strong so that I may give away my small self, and make me weak so I may learn to love the vulnerability of silence.

Notes

Journey

Day 13

REAL STRUGGLE HURTS. IT MARKS us in ways we don't even always realize when it happens. Years can pass before we begin to comprehend the marks and scars trouble hews out of the flesh of our lives. It leaves us wounded and chastened and different for the rest of our days. "After he died," we hear a woman say, "I was never the same again." When I didn't get the position," we hear a professional say, "it took the heart right out of me. I lost interest in everything." "When I couldn't go to college," we hear a young person say, "I stopped kidding myself that I'd ever be anything in life." "When we split up," we're told, "my life ended." Struggle brings us to crossover points in life after which we become new people, sometimes worse, often better, but always different.

There is no hiding from struggle. It takes place deep down inside of us, in that tender place from which there is no refuge. No external enemy is nearly as demanding, as damaging, as destructive as the enemy within, the one of our own making. It is our own lust or pride or greed or jealousy or anger or gluttony or envy that takes us down… It is our innate compassion and humility and self-knowledge and largesse and justice and courage that call us to become our better selves. It is in the crucible of struggle that one of these outweighs the other, not always and not only, but often. In fact, is there anywhere other than struggle that they can really come to bloom?

᷑

BIBLICAL WISDOM

I urge you, . . . by our Lord Jesus Christ and by the love of the Spirit, to join me in my struggle by praying to God for me. Romans 15:30

SILENCE FOR MEDITATION

QUESTIONS TO PONDER

- How does your faith community help its members deal creatively with struggles? Could it do any better? If so, how?

- What are the benefits of struggle? What are its wounds or hurts?
- What does Joan Chittister mean by "the enemy within"? Is it an enemy that can be fought alone? How can others help in the struggle?

PSALM FRAGMENTS

Be gracious to me, O God, for people trample on me;
*   all day long foes oppress me;*
my enemies trample on me all day long,
*   for many fight against me.*
O Most High, when I am afraid,
*   I put my trust in you.* Psalm 56:2-3

JOURNAL REFLECTIONS

- Meditate on the "crossover points" in your life that struggle has brought you to. As a result of the struggle, how did you change? Did you become "worse" or "better"? Why?
- Have you identified the shape of your own "enemy within"? What gives you courage to confront and transform that enemy? Who helps you in the struggle?
- List what have been "the marks and scars trouble hews out of the flesh of our lives" in your experience. Does healing feel possible? Why or why not?

PRAYERS OF HOPE & HEALING

Pray for all those who are struggling today, that God will give them the strength and the courage to go on. Pray that the hearts of humanity will bring solace to the most impoverished and hopeless among us, healing the wounds of neglect and unconcern. May our commitment to nonviolence and compassion exceed our desire for retribution, possession, and fear.

PRAYER FOR TODAY

In every struggle, dear God, you have bound me to your heart. Help me to learn from my trials and sufferings the power of your love.

NOTES

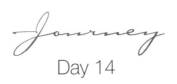

Day 14

It is a great burden to be perfect. The fear of failure skulks around the perimeters of hubris with irritating constancy. There is always the possibility that someone will come along who is even more perfect than we are. There is, if nothing else, the weight of being responsible for the world by those who think they are. Unable to accept ourselves as we are, we wear ourselves out in an effort to become unimpeachable.

Fortunately, we are spared the problems that come with perfection because none of us is. Not me; not you. It is, unfortunately, the strain of discovering the benefits of imperfection that takes so much time and effort in life. Every stage of life is a matter of trial and error. In each one there is something to be learned the hard way. The tendency is to approach them with naiveté, if not depreciation, and leave them with wisdom… The paradox is that to be human is to be imperfect but it is exactly our imperfection that is our claim to the best of the human condition. We are not a sorry lot. We have one another. We are not expected to be self-sufficient. It is precisely our vulnerability that entitles us to love and guarantees us a hearing from the rest of the human race.

BIBLICAL WISDOM

In the same way, the Spirit helps us in our weakness. We do not know what we ought to pray for, but the Spirit intercedes for us with groans that words cannot express. Romans 8:26

SILENCE FOR MEDITATION

QUESTIONS TO PONDER

- The quest for perfection and personal or social violence often go together. What are the spiritual implications of an excessive quest for perfection?
- What does Joan Chittister mean by the "benefits of imperfection"?

- Describe how trial and error and the acceptance of both failure and success can lead to the "best of the human condition."
- In what way might an awareness of "our vulnerability" become the foundation for great spiritual strength? Consider examples in your own experience and in social or political situations.

PSALM FRAGMENTS

He has pity on the weak and the needy,
and saves the lives of the needy.
From oppression and violence he redeems their life;
and precious is their blood in his sight. Psalm 72:13-14

JOURNAL REFLECTIONS

- Do you have a tendency toward perfectionism? If so, how does it affect your spiritual health?
- In what ways might acknowledging imperfection and/or vulnerability help you to open yourself to others and receive their gifts of love? Meditate on the ways in which lack of self-sufficiency becomes a crucible for spiritual wisdom.
- Meditate on whether you feel most loved and accepted when you acknowledge your vulnerability and all it means or when you resist it.

PRAYERS OF HOPE & HEALING

Pray for the most vulnerable among us that the heart of humanity will overflow with compassion and wisdom. Pray for your family and friends that they will be receptive to how interdependent and vulnerable our bodies, minds, and spirits are. Pray that "vulnerability" will be experienced as a strength beyond understanding, the strength of the Spirit in us.

PRAYER FOR TODAY

Allow me to be gentle with myself. Allow me to savor my humanness and my limitations. Allow me, Holy One, to fall into your arms.

NOTES

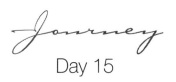

Day 15

FREEDOM IS THE CAPSTONE OF truth. Our time is short here and there is much to do. Therefore, we must cultivate a passion for the truth. We must seek it, demand it, and tell it. And once we have broken through the levels of propriety and protocol that collude to pretend that what isn't true is necessary, we are forever free. No one can ever enslave us again.

Self-esteem is the blessing that comes with honesty. With self-esteem we cannot lose, no matter what we lose. Longfellow's lines hold immortal value: "Those that respect themselves are safe from others; they wear a coat of mail that none can pierce." When we have done what must be done, what we were put here to do at this time, in this age, at this place, then we can live with heads up and hearts unbroken, whatever our losses. Then no one can best us, even when we fail the fray. Then we will never die before we have lived.

This time, indeed, is the only time to be born. On it, in fact, depend the two pillars of my life: my freedom of soul and my eternal self-esteem.

~

BIBLICAL WISDOM

Now the Lord is the Spirit, and where the Spirit of the Lord is, there is freedom.
 2 Corinthians 3:17

SILENCE FOR MEDITATION

QUESTIONS TO PONDER

- Why does Joan Chittister argue that freedom is the "capstone," or *crowning achievement,* of truth?
- Does your community of faith help you to "cultivate a passion for the truth" or not? What would such a passion look like?
- If "the levels of propriety and protocol…collude to pretend that what isn't

true is necessary," it seems that the guardian of "propriety and protocol"—organized religion—might find itself actually against the passion for truth and the freedom it brings. Do you see this as a practical problem for organized religion? If so, what can be done? If not, why not?

PSALM FRAGMENTS

Let them praise his name with dancing,
  making melody to him with tambourine and lyre.
For the LORD takes pleasure in his people;
  he adorns the humble with victory. Psalm 149:3-4

JOURNAL REFLECTIONS

- Meditate on the ways you have cultivated personally a passion for truth. Do you feel that your quest for truth has strengthened your character and deepened your soul?
- Reflect on how your own search for freedom and self-respect has affected your relationships and community. What aspects of this search have been most difficult; most rewarding?
- In your journal, write a list of the experiences that have (1) fostered or (2) taken away your freedom and self-respect. How has your soul reacted to these experiences? What have you learned from them?

PRAYERS OF HOPE & HEALING

Pray for a greater deepening of freedom, and a greater longing to know your self through the eyes of the Spirit. Pray that the troubled and pained in your own heart and in the heart of the world will be healed by the grace of God's love. Pray that the gifts of "freedom of the soul" and "eternal self-esteem" will be the true inheritance of the spirit for you, your family, and friends—indeed, for all people.

PRAYER FOR TODAY

Enflame me, Beloved, with the Holy Spirit's fire, and set me free from bondage. May your freedom become the emblem of my devotion.

NOTES

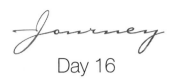

Day 16

WEEPING, IN FACT, MAY BE the best indicator we have of what life is really all about for us. It may be only when we weep that we can come to know best either ourselves or our worlds. What we weep for measures what we are. What we weep over indicates what others may expect of us in life. It was when Jesus wept over Jerusalem that the die was cast, not for crucifixion, but for the blaze of energy and the boldness of stature that spent everything in him to change what, in the end, though it could not be changed, could not be ignored either. Tears, you see, are more than sadness...

Of all the expressions of human emotion in the lexicon of life, weeping may be the most functional, the most deeply versatile. The tears we weep show us our deepest, neediest, most private selves. Our tears expose us. They lay us bare both to others and to ourselves. What we cry about is what we care about. What we have no tears for hardens our hearts.

⌁

BIBLICAL WISDOM

So I weep, as Jazer weeps, for the vines of Sibmah. O Heshbon, O Elealeh, I drench you with tears! The shouts of joy over your ripened fruit and over your harvests have been stilled. Isaiah 16:9

SILENCE FOR MEDITATION

QUESTIONS TO PONDER

- Is weeping culturally valued or disparaged? Why?
- In what ways does your faith community either facilitate or hinder weeping over both your own or others' suffering and sorrow and joys and celebrations?
- Would you agree that "what we weep for measures what we are"? Why or why not?

Psalm Fragments

Those who go out weeping,
bearing the seed for sowing,
shall come home with shouts of joy,
carrying their sheaves. Psalm 126:6

Journal Reflections

- Make a list of people, things, events that you weep over?
- In your journal, reflect on how and to whom you reveal your "deepest, neediest, most private" self. What feelings arise in allowing yourself to cry and lay bare your soul?
- If "what we cry about is what we care about [and] what we have no tears for hardens our hearts," what do you care about and where has your heart been hardened?

Prayers of Hope & Healing

Pray that our hearts will be touched by the beauty of creation, and that our tears will bring healing to all those who suffer. Pray for the capacity to weep and for the capacity to shed tears. May our deepest, most private selves find hope in the sensitivity of relations.

Prayer for Today

As I weep with tears of fire, may the love of the Divine soothe my weary soul.

Notes

Journey

Day 17

PEACE COMES WHEN WE KNOW that there is something that the Spirit
has to teach us in everything we do, in everything we experience. When
we are rejected, we learn that there is a love above all loves in life. When
we are afraid, we come to know that there are those who will take care
of us whatever the cost to themselves. When we are lonely, we learn that
there is a rich and vibrant world inside us waiting to be explored if we
will only make the effort.

When we are threatened by differences, we come to realize that the
gift of the other is grace in disguise meant to broaden the narrowness that
constricts our souls. Then peace comes, then quiet sets in; then there is
nothing that anyone can do to us that can destroy that equilibrium, upset
our inner balance. What is, is, that's true. But what is, we come to see, is
that God's world is good in all its dimensions. When I finally plumb my
own depths, take the measure of myself, find the world within me that
is spirit and light and truth, what is outside of me can never destroy my
centered self.

~

BIBLICAL WISDOM

*Peace I leave with you; my peace I give you. I do not give to you as the world
gives. Do not let your hearts be troubled and do not be afraid.* John 14:27

SILENCE FOR MEDITATION

QUESTIONS TO PONDER

- If "there is something that the Spirit has to teach us in everything we do,
  in everything we experience," how can we become open to this teaching?
- In what ways can a community of faith help people open themselves to the
  Spirit's teaching?
- With all of the violence and suffering in the world, how could it make
  sense to say: "God's world is good in all its dimensions"?

Psalm Fragments

Search me, O God, and know my heart;
 test me and know my thoughts.
See if there is any wicked way in me,
 and lead me in the way everlasting. Psalm 139:23-24

Journal Reflections

- Contemplate how and in what way inner peace comes to you. Write about what brings greater peace to you and what takes peace away.
- Choose one of your life experiences in which you believe the Spirit was teaching you. What did you learn? Has the learning stayed with you? Have you experienced greater inner peace as a result?
- Joan Chittister encourages us to "plumb [our] own depths, take the measure of [ourselves], find the world within [us] that is spirit and light and truth…" Reflect on your own spiritual life. Where are you on this journey? Have you found your "centered self"?

Prayers of Hope & Healing

Pray for the serenity that only a pure heart can hold. Pray for the wisdom to find the Spirit in every life situation so that each day you grow in love. Pray for determination and passion so you may be healed of all that narrows or constricts your soul.

Prayer for Today

Teach me, O Peace, how to be quiet and strong in myself. Grant me the serenity of wisdom, so that I may remember that God alone sustains the fluttering of my heart.

Notes

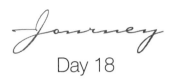

Day 18

IN A WORLD OF ROLE definitions and a theology of gender, sexual stereotypes are built right into the spiritual life. The whole idea that God will work through some facets of creation, but not through others, defies the whole definition of God. Even more than that, it ignores the science of difference. Difference is the very dynamic of creation. It is difference that makes life possible, that gives life variety, that demonstrates the glory of God in all its facets. But instead of seeing differences as a sign of the limitlessness of God's presence and God's power, we have allowed them to be confined and controlled.

Clearly, our degree of commitment to the emergence of feminist spirituality marks the quality of our spiritual lives. We can go on forming people in the molds that make a patriarchal system run or we can let loose the Holy Spirit to sweep dangerously through the world. We can commit ourselves to bringing out the strengths in ourselves by admitting the weaknesses in us, in men as well as women, until we are all a creation in full concert with the creator. The suppression of women is a sin, not because it is a sin against women, but because it is a sin against creation itself. To suppress half of God's creation in the name of God is a sin against the Holy Spirit for which we have no name.

⁓

BIBLICAL WISDOM

For now we see in a mirror dimly, but then face to face. Now I know in part; then I shall understand fully, even as I have been fully understood. 1 Corinthians 13:12

SILENCE FOR MEDITATION

Questions to Ponder

- In what way are "sexual stereotypes . . . built right into the spiritual life"?
- Do you agree that both popular culture and religious institutions form "people in the molds that make a patriarchal system"? What is the evidence?
- What would we (individuals and faith communities) need to do to "let loose the Holy Spirit to sweep dangerously through the world"?

Psalm Fragments

The earth is the Lord's and all that is in it,
the world, and those who live in it;
for he has founded it on the seas,
*   and established it on the rivers.* Psalm 24:1-2

Journal Reflections

- Meditate on how God celebrates differences in creation.
- Write about the ways that females and the feminine have been suppressed in your own life; in societies, religions, and nations.
- Contemplate your "degree of commitment to the emergence of feminist spirituality."

Prayers of Hope & Healing

Pray for women and girls everywhere that they will someday know the fullness of their humanity and beauty. Pray for women and men that the feminine in creation will be allowed to flourish, allowed to *be*. Pray for the healing of hearts and the healing of minds, bodies, and spirits so that the ancient and historical denigration of women finally will be released.

Prayer for Today

God, your creation is full of splendor and mystery! May your compassion heal my spiritual wounds and help me honor the beauty of my difference.

Notes

Day 19

IF GOD IS ANYWHERE, THE greatest writers of the spiritual life have taught for centuries, God is in us, bringing us to life, drawing us incessantly on to that place where we become everything we can be. The soul, that place where the human meets the divine, lives to develop the God-life in us here and now, to be light whatever the darkness that surrounds us, to bring us to a sense of self that satisfies without subsuming everything else in its path. The posture of the soul before a God who dwells in the heart of us to give us life, to give us peace, to give us security is at once a profound bow and at the same time a wide-open embrace of the universe. It is a mix of audacious humility and diffident pride that gives the lie to everything we've ever been told to the contrary about both.

To be immersed in God implies an accommodation with life that is less than perfect, acceptance of a world that is not organized around my ego, satisfaction with a self that is not measured by its ascendancy over others. When God becomes the core of my soul, the energy of my life, the end of my actions, the measure of my needs, every other relationship, every other perspective shifts accordingly.

~

BIBLICAL WISDOM

Love the Lord your God with all your heart and with all your soul and with all your strength. Deuteronomy 6:5

SILENCE FOR MEDITATION

QUESTIONS TO PONDER

- Does your community of faith help you to recognize that "God is in us, drawing us incessantly" toward union and intimacy? Is there anything the community of faith could do to better help?
- If the soul is "that place where human meets divine," how might *soul mates*

or *spiritual friends* help each other "to develop the God-life in [each other] here and now"?

- If God were to become the core of your soul and the center of your life, actions, and needs, how might your relationships change and grow?

Psalm Fragments

Bless the LORD, O my soul.
O LORD my God, you are very great.
You are clothed with honor and majesty,
wrapped in light as with a garment. Psalm 104:1-2b

Journal Reflections

- Describe the "posture of [your] soul before God." In what way do you foster time for prayer and reflection, for meeting God in your own heart?
- Meditate on your soul's needs at this time. What might you do to meet those needs that you are not already doing?
- Do you have a soul mate or spiritual friend? If so, in what ways are she or he helpful in your spiritual life and you in theirs? If not, would you like one? What might you do to build such a relationship?

Prayers of Hope & Healing

Pray for humanity that God—by whatever name—will be discovered within. Pray that this meeting of divine and human leads to the transformation of our hearts and the renewal of creation. Offer a prayer for your family and spiritual community that the divine will draw them ever closer to hope, faith, and compassion.

Prayer for Today

May your dark light of wisdom penetrate my soul and help me to long for you more each day. It is for you, God, that my parched soul thirsts.

Notes

Journey

Day 20

IN ORDER TO LAY TO rest the theology of indirect redemption that has plagued the misunderstood humanity of women, it is time for the Church to speak plainly, boldly, and clearly its acceptance of woman as a full human being. In a very special way, the woman's issue is the most radical of justice issues. If the case can be made that one kind of human, the woman, is genetically inferior and disposed by nature to a state of subjugation, then domination is clearly part of the creative scheme. If women are less than men, so different as to be incompetent, so unreasonable as to be incapable, then it is a very short step to the justified napalming of Orientals, the lynching of blacks, and the extermination of Indians because, it can be argued, the Creator God built inferiority right into the human race…

Sincere but false pieties have been the basis for women's inferior status throughout history; it is the kind of piety, baseless to content and evil in effect, that the Church must now confront if it is to grow to the fullness of Christ. And this demands that the Church educate to equality, raise women's expectations of themselves, and be a model for human justice. We cannot continue to separate roles and responsibilities on the basis of sex. We cannot define womanhood by motherhood unless we are also willing to define manhood by fatherhood. We cannot counsel people into bondage.

BIBLICAL WISDOM

Jesus turned and saw her. "Take heart, daughter," he said, "your faith has healed you." And the woman was healed from that moment. Matthew 9:22

SILENCE FOR MEDITATION

QUESTIONS TO PONDER

• Do you feel it is the duty of the Church to "speak plainly, boldly, and clearly of its acceptance of woman as a full human being"? In what way is this issue the "most radical of justice issues"?

- Why is it theologically untenable for societies and religions to promote the subjugation and disenfranchisement of women?
- How can individuals and communities of faith "be a model for human justice"? What immediate steps must be taken to ensure the full equality of women and girls?

PSALM FRAGMENTS

O LORD, how manifold are your works!
   In wisdom you have made them all;
   the earth is full of your creatures. Psalm 104:24

JOURNAL REFLECTIONS

- Meditate on the subtle and overt ways that your religious community and/ or social relations endorse oppression. How does this make your heart and soul feel?
- Contemplate the ways in which the feminine spirit is damaged or subjugated in you, whether you are male or female. Write about steps you can take to change this.
- Do you feel you harbor a consciousness of oppression? Meditate on ways to free your consciousness from old patterns of reaction and behavior.

PRAYERS OF HOPE & HEALING

Pray for your community of faith that the theology of gender will be transformed into a theology of equality. Offer a prayer that the feminine will be healed and will become ever more present in today's world. Pray for our leaders that they may grow in wisdom and become "a model for human justice."

PRAYER FOR TODAY

O God of justice and peace! Please open my heart and the hearts of all humanity to the suffering of women and the subjugation of the feminine spirit of life.

NOTES

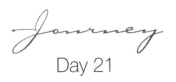

Day 21

PEOPLE WHO ARE REALLY HUMBLE, who know themselves to be earth or humus—the root from which our word "humble" comes—have about themselves an air of self-containment and self-control. There's no haughtiness, no distance, no sarcasm, no put downs, no airs of importance or disdain. The ability to deal with both their own limitations and the limitations of others, the recognition that God is in life and that they are not in charge of the universe brings serenity and hope, inner peace and real energy. Humble people walk comfortably in every group. No one is either beneath them or too above them for their own sense of well-being…

Humility is not a false recognition of God's gifts. To exaggerate the gifts we have by denying them may be as close to narcissism as we can get in life. No, humility is the admission of God's gifts to me and the acknowledgement that I have been given them for others. Humility is the total continuing surrender to God's power in my life and in the lives of those around me.

༄

BIBLICAL WISDOM

If my people, who are called by my name, will humble themselves and pray and seek my face and turn from their wicked ways, then will I hear from heaven and will forgive their sin and will heal their land. 2 Chronicles 7:14

SILENCE FOR MEDITATION

QUESTIONS TO PONDER

- What attitudes in our culture promote arrogance and self-importance rather than humility?
- What are the virtues of a humble heart? How can they be applied in everyday situations, in political or religious life?
- Institutions—like individuals—can be either humble or haughty. How would you rate the religious institutions you are a part of? Why?

PSALM FRAGMENTS

He leads the humble in what is right,
and teaches the humble his way. Psalm 25:9

JOURNAL REFLECTIONS

- Do you consider yourself a humble person? Why or why not?
- Contemplate God's gifts to you that might be used for others. Do you use them for others? If so, in what ways? If not, what stops you?
- List people you know who are genuinely humble. What is it about them that you find attractive? What can you learn from them?

PRAYERS OF HOPE & HEALING

Offer a prayer for your family, spiritual friends, and colleagues, that their hearts will grow in true humbleness and gratitude for God's gifts. Pray for your nation that its leaders recognize that "they are not in charge of the universe." In your heart say a prayer of "serenity...hope [and] inner peace" for the wonders of life itself.

PRAYER FOR TODAY

Help me, Loving Creator, to accept your gifts in me with a humble heart. May I honor my limitations and the limitations of others as I grow in peace and serenity.

NOTES

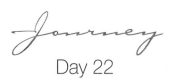

Day 22

HOSPITALITY MEANS WE TAKE PEOPLE into our space that is our lives and our minds and our hearts and our world and our efforts. Hospitality is the way we come out of ourselves. It is the first step toward dismantling the barriers of the world. Hospitality is the way we turn a prejudiced world around, one heart at a time.

There will be racism in the world until you and I begin to take the other races in. There will be war, until you and I begin to take the enemy in. There will be classism, until you and I begin to take the other segments of society into our own worlds and lives and parties and neighborhoods.

The Rule of Benedict is a tonic for human separations. Benedict takes in the poor and the pilgrim, the young and the old, the rich and the deprived, the ones of our own family of faith and the passersby. And every guest is received with the same warmth and the same care, the same dignity and the same attention.

BIBLICAL WISDOM

Beloved, you do faithfully whatever you do for the friends, even though they are strangers to you; . . . Therefore we ought to show hospitality to such people, so that we may become co-workers with the truth. 3 John 1:5, 8

SILENCE FOR MEDITATION

QUESTIONS TO PONDER

- How effective is the ministry of hospitality in your community of faith; in other institutions of which you are a part? How might hospitality be improved?
- Think about hospitality as a way of being, a basic stance towards others. How can it be taught and practiced?

- Think of hospitality as "the way we turn a prejudiced world around." Think about our world. Why does there seem to be so much prejudice?

PSALM FRAGMENTS

Hear my prayer, O LORD,
and give ear to my cry;
do not hold your peace at my tears.
For I am your passing guest,
an alien, like all my forebears. Psalm 39:12

JOURNAL REFLECTIONS

- Would you describe yourself as a hospitable person? Why or why not?
- Reflect on those times in your life when you were received with true hospitality. How did it make you feel?
- Meditate on receiving every person—rich and deprived, young and old—with "the same warmth and the same care, the same dignity and the same attention." In what ways would this change your life?

PRAYERS OF HOPE & HEALING

Pray for the healing of prejudice "one heart at a time." Pray that the joy of hospitality will grow in the hearts of our young people and help our world to be more caring and patient. May our hearts open to take in and experience the aloneness, separation, and loneliness of the "other."

PRAYER FOR TODAY

May your light shine on me, Holy One, until my soul is made humble and free. Take me and use me for your work of reconciliation in the world.

NOTES

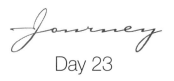

Day 23

THE REAL PROBLEM WITH CHANGE is that it means the undoing of what went before it. That kind of revisionism is hard enough in the business world where people come and go between one job and another, between the office and a family life somewhere else. It is even harder when it involves the sensitivities of a living community, all of whose members have lived the past for varying degrees of time, in varying intensities, with varying measures of similarity between life as they knew it before they entered the convent and life as they went on living it there.

The renewal of religious life did not simply involve a community's willingness to adopt a checklist of new behaviors. It required that religious cease to do a number of things that had been considered eternal, thought of as absolutes, once assumed were the ultimate norms of sanctity. Renewal, suddenly, harked back to the author of Ecclesiastes simply but profoundly, "There is a time for tearing down and a time for building up."

BIBLICAL WISDOM

If you really change your ways and your actions and deal with each other justly, if you do not oppress the alien, the fatherless, or the widow and do not shed innocent blood in this place, . . . then I will let you live in this place, in the land I gave your forefathers for ever and ever. Jeremiah 7:5-7

SILENCE FOR MEDITATION

Questions to Ponder

- In the context of your faith community, describe what it means to change "things that had been considered eternal, thought of as absolutes, once assumed were the ultimate norms of sanctity"?
- If you have you experienced this kind of change, describe its impact on your own life and faith, and the life and faith of your spiritual community.
- Why is change often difficult and painful for groups and communities? What advice would you give a person (or a community) who is undergoing radical transformation?

Psalm Fragments

When you send forth your spirit, they are created;
and you renew the face of the ground. Psalm 104:30

Journal Reflections

- Meditate on the passage from Ecclesiastes: "There is a time for tearing down and a time for building up." From the standpoint of your faith, what "time" are you in now? What are you doing about it?
- Do you tend to resist change or welcome it? Why?
- Have you experienced the difficulty of the "undoing of what went before"? If so, describe the experience and its outcome?

Prayers of Hope & Healing

Open your heart and pray for the Spirit to dwell within the painful and joyful changes in life. Pray for the courage to face the "time for tearing down" and the fortitude to capture "the time for building up." Pray that light shines on and transforms the "absolutes" and "eternals" in thought and institutions that wound and oppress.

Prayer for Today

Console me, Divine Mother, as the storms of change tear down my limitations and build up my longing for your life. Grant me the courage of faith.

Notes

"IN MY WEAKNESS IS MY strength," Paul writes (2 Cor 12:10). I never understood that passage nor did I like it until, struck with polio as a young woman, I began little by little to realize that if I ever walked again, it would not be thanks to me, it would be thanks to everyone around me who formed the human chain that kept me human. When I could not move, they carried me. When I could not work, they found functions for me that justified my existence. When I could not find a reason for going on, they liked me enough to give me back a sense of human connectedness. When I could not cure myself, they cured me of the clay of my limits and turned them into life again. They taught me the glories of weakness for both of us.

When I most of all wanted to be strong and like no other time in life found myself defined by my weaknesses, I began to understand the great question of life. If I do not need other people, what can I ever learn? And if I do not need other people, what is their own purpose in life, what is their claim on my own gifts when they need me as I have needed them? The moment I come to realize that it is precisely the gifts which I do not myself embody that make me claimant to the gifts of others—and they of mine—marks the moment of my spiritual beginning. Suddenly, creature-hood becomes gift and power and the beginning of unlimited personal growth.

⌐

BIBLICAL WISDOM

But he said to me, "My grace is sufficient for you, for my power is made perfect in weakness." Therefore I will boast all the more gladly about my weaknesses, so that Christ's power may rest on me. 2 Corinthians 12:9

SILENCE FOR MEDITATION

Questions to Ponder

- In what ways can a faith community form "the human chain that keeps us human" when our own strength and abilities are inadequate to the situations we face?
- What does it mean to see life in community as an interdependence of gifts?
- What do we learn by needing other people?

Psalm Fragments

How very good and pleasant it is
when kindred live together in unity! Psalm 133:1

Journal Reflections

- Reflect on how weakness is celebrated in this passage. In your journal, write about your own experiences of weakness and what strength you found in them.
- Meditate on the ways in which your own weaknesses have led you closer to or further from the affirmation of life.
- List the gifts provided to you by people, the natural world, and the Spirit. Write about your essential need for and interdependence with these gifts.

Prayers of Hope & Healing

Pray for the healing of arrogance and self-sufficiency. Pray for the community of beings that we may grow more aware of our mutual need and interdependence. Pray that the heart of humanity will open to "the beginning of unlimited personal growth."

Prayer for Today

Dear God, I know you are with me in my strength and in my weakness. Show me how to celebrate weakness as a sign of growth into your heart.

Notes

Day 25

"A RIGHT," PAST ATTORNEY GENERAL Ramsey Clarke said, "Is not something…anyone can give you. A right is something that no one can take away." Men cannot "give" women their human rights. They can only agree not to take them away. Those rights go with being human. They are inalienable, inherent, unarguable. Now. But not always. Not for everyone. The white Western world never really recognized the concept of universal human rights for centuries. And even after the Enlightenment, there were still questions about Indians, about blacks, about women. The first questions contested their full humanity. Only later, only now, are some peoples even beginning to ask about the rights that the mere fact of being human implies for women as well as for men…

It's 1995 and we still need to argue the point for women. We still need documents asserting the situation for women. That ought to tell us something about the way the world goes together. That ought to say something to people who still "Tsk, tsk" over the Women's Movement. The Women's Movement is not asking for the destruction of men; it's asking for the human recognition of women—for the full recognition of women as humans!

BIBLICAL WISDOM

Blessed are they who maintain justice, who constantly do what is right. Psalm 106:3

SILENCE FOR MEDITATION

QUESTIONS TO PONDER

- What are human rights? Why are they "inalienable, inherent, unarguable"? Why are they "not something anyone can give you"?
- If "a right is something that no one can take away," what does it mean to say that men must "agree not to take them away" from women?

- How would worship and religions be different if the "full recognition of women as humans" were acknowledged and upheld?

PSALM FRAGMENTS

They crush your people, O LORD,
and afflict your heritage.
They kill the widow and the stranger,
they murder the orphan,
and they say, "The LORD does not see;
the God of Jacob does not perceive."
Understand, O dullest of the people;
fools, when will you be wise?
He who planted the ear, does he not hear?
He who formed the eye, does he not see? Psalm 94:5-9

JOURNAL REFLECTIONS

- Do you feel that any of your rights as a human being are being ignored or blatantly disregarded? If so, what does it feel like? If not, can you imagine what it might feel like to others?
- Would you consider the freedom to lead a full spiritual life to be a human right? Do men and women have equal freedom in this area? Do you have this freedom? Why or why not?
- Whether you are a woman or a man, have you witnessed (or participated in) the denial of basic human rights to women and girls? If so, what did you do (or what might you do in the future)?

PRAYERS OF HOPE & HEALING

Pray for the continued administration of rights for women, men, and all creation. Pray for the healing of possession, control, and superiority that generates the denial of women's rights around the world. Pray that the inalienable gifts granted by our Creator to humans and nature will lead to renewed hope for our planet.

PRAYER FOR TODAY

May my heart overflow with compassion for the suffering of humanity everywhere. Help me, Jesus, to practice nonviolence of spirit.

NOTES

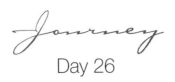

Day 26

THE WOMEN STANDING BESIDE THE peace candle in the front of the auditorium, some draped in chadors, some dressed in pantsuits, were a mixed gathering, some Israeli, some Arab…all of whom had lost family members in the conflict: Israeli mothers who had lost their sons in the army, a twenty-year-old Palestinian girl whose fiancé had been recently killed by errant Israeli gunfire, a Palestinian women from East Jerusalem who lost her sister in the conflict.

But none of them spoke about anger, revenge, justice, or security fences. They spoke simply about the fact that it was the other—the mother of the Israeli son speaking to the mother of the Palestinian child, the Palestinian sister listening to the grief of the Israeli mother—whose presence, understanding, mutual grief, and lingering pain brought peace and healing to each of them.

These women had simply moved beyond the rest of us… Indeed, these women had all been to Mount Moriah, and they knew in their grief, heard in their hearts, what so many others had failed to understand or refused to hear. They knew . . . that [not] even the will of God was worth one hair on the head of one child.

ↄ

BIBLICAL WISDOM

The Lord said, "I have indeed seen the misery of my people in Egypt. I have heard them crying out because of their slave drivers, and I am concerned about their suffering. Exodus 3:7

SILENCE FOR MEDITATION

QUESTIONS TO PONDER

- Do you agree "that [not] even the will of God [is] worth one hair on the head of one child"? Why or why not?

- If it is true "that [not] even the will of God [is] worth one hair on the head of one child," then how do you explain all the religiously motivated and sanctioned violence in the world?
- How can we facilitate the coming together of "enemies" to share their grief over the violence and death they have experienced?

PSALM FRAGMENTS

May the LORD give you increase,
both you and your children.
May you be blessed by the LORD,
who made heaven and earth. Psalm 115:14-15

JOURNAL REFLECTIONS

- Meditate on your experiences of loss. Have you ever shared your grief with those who are seen as responsible for it? If so, write about the experience. If not, image what the experience might be like.
- Write about how your own grief or pain has brought you to a greater understanding of another's suffering.
- Write about the ways in which feeling another's pain as your own brought about peace and healing to a relationship.

PRAYERS OF HOPE & HEALING

Offer prayers for the women, men, and children displaced and without food or shelter in war-torn regions of the world. Pray that the citizens of our planet will reach out in hope and healing to alleviate the suffering of the least among us. Pray that "your presence, understanding, mutual grief, and lingering pain" will bring peace and healing.

PRAYER FOR TODAY

Divine Mother of us all, help my heart and the heart of our world to clamor for peace. In the name of suffering humanity everywhere, lament with us and show us the way to healing.

NOTES

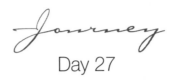

Day 27

CONFUCIUS TAUGHT THAT THERE ARE three methods by which we can learn wisdom: through thought, through imitation, through experience... Thought, Confucius implied, gives foundation to action. Unless I have thought through the values to be gained in any situation, I choose blindly. The one who is enlightened chooses consciously for altruism over profit, for depth of soul over the hoarding of things, for emptiness rather than a glut of superficial distractions that can only separate us from ourselves.

Imitation, Confucius reminds us, reveals what we assess is good. The people after whom we shape our own lives, the people who are our heroes, provide the clue to our own value system.

Experience, Confucius teaches, guides us through life at its dregs and provides the final test of enlightenment. Who we are on the other side of pain and loss is who we are at our best.

BIBLICAL WISDOM

Does not wisdom call, and does not understanding raise her voice? On the heights, beside the way, at the crossroads she takes her stand; beside the gates in front of the town, at the entrance of the portals she cries out: "To you, O people, I call, and my cry is to all that live. O simple ones, learn prudence; acquire intelligence, you who lack it. Proverbs 8:1-5

SILENCE FOR MEDITATION

QUESTIONS TO PONDER

- If a faith community were to practice Confucius' three methods of learning wisdom, how would they order their relations?
- What kinds of similarities exist between the wisdom of Confucius and the wisdom of Jesus? Are there differences?

- Which of the three methods—thought, imitation, experience—is most difficult? Why?

PSALM FRAGMENTS

You desire truth in the inward being;
therefore teach me wisdom in my secret heart. Psalm 51: 6

JOURNAL REFLECTIONS

- What might be the value of applying the three "methods" for learning wisdom to your own life? Do you find "thought, imitation, and experience" to be cornerstones of your spiritual development? If so, in what ways? If not, why not?
- In your journal, contemplate the spiritual importance of choosing "altruism over profit, depth of soul over hoarding of things, [and] emptiness rather than a glut of superficial distractions."
- Write about an experience of pain and loss. What was learned as a result of the experience? Were you a better person because of it?

PRAYERS OF HOPE & HEALING

Offer prayers of simplicity, that we may learn the value of impermanence. Offer prayers of joy, that we may discover the beauty of letting go. Offer prayers of healing, that all souls will come to know peace.

PRAYER FOR TODAY

Divine Spirit, each day as I practice the three methods of Confucius for learning wisdom, increase my longing to learn the final tests, to be my best on the other side of pain and loss.

NOTES

Journey

Day 28

BENEDICTINE ASCETICISM IS SCRIPTURAL AND communal and committed to psychological and spiritual adulthood. To develop a Benedictine spirituality means to reject a static concept of perfection in which keeping the rules and going through the motions is, at best, an easy way. Benedictine spirituality plunges me into human relations that are meant to reveal the will of God to me, to call forth the best in me, to be a source of support and a measure of my personal responsibility. Perhaps the best test of the reality of these in my life is a simple question: In the last three things that bothered me this week, whom did I blame and was it really worth the emotional energy I give to it?

Benedictine conversion, then, is not an assertion of our strength of character. Benedictine spirituality is based on the simple acknowledgement that God will come to life before us and be reborn in us in unexpected ways day after day throughout our lives. We must be ready to respond to this God of woods and highways, of gentle breeze and cataclysm, of privacy and crowds—however this Spirit comes.

BIBLICAL WISDOM

As soon as Jesus was baptized, he went up out of the water. At that moment heaven was opened, and he saw the Spirit of God descending like a dove and lighting on him. Matthew 3:16

SILENCE FOR MEDITATION

QUESTIONS TO PONDER

- In a community of faith, why would "keeping the rules and going through the motions" be the easy way, but not the right way?
- What would it mean to a faith community to be "committed to psychological and spiritual adulthood"? Do you find evidence of such a com-

mitment in your faith community? If so, where? If not, what can you do about it?

- In what ways can a community of faith help its people "to respond to this God of woods and highways, of gentle breeze and cataclysm, of privacy and crowds" outside the four walls of institutional religion?

PSALM FRAGMENTS

Our God comes and does not keep silence,
  before him is a devouring fire,
  and a mighty tempest all around him. Psalm 50:6

JOURNAL REFLECTIONS

- List your key human relationships. In what ways do these relationships "reveal the will of God to [you]" and "call forth the best in [you]?
- "In the last three things that bothered [you] this week, whom did [you] blame and was it really worth the emotional energy [you] give to it"?
- Meditate on some of the unexpected ways in which God has come to life before you and been born within you. How might you make yourself more open to such experiences?

PRAYERS OF HOPE & HEALING

Pray to be free from emotional distractions and physical demands. Pray to learn how to dwell in silence with your God. Pray for our religious sisters and brothers that the Spirit will heal and transform through their efforts.

PRAYER FOR TODAY

Come to life in me, each day, Holy One. Help me to turn all my worries over to the Spirit who fills the universe with joy.

NOTES

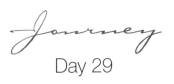

Day 29

IT IS NOT NECESSARY TO withdraw from the world in order to be holy. In fact, it may be more difficult to make a spiritual case for withdrawal than it is to understand creative immersion in the world around us. Otherwise, how do we explain the Jesus who walked from Galilee to Jerusalem, curing lepers, giving sight to the blind, raising women from the dead? Does Jesus qualify as a contemplative or not? And if so, then surely withdrawal is not the only way to get to be one.

We must learn that life itself is of God, that the natural is sacred, and that an inward life and immersion in life are of a piece. If we are in God, then all of life becomes sacred to us. To seek God means to find God around us. The God-questions propel us into life, in fact. It is precisely when we begin to see the world through the eyes of God that life becomes the measure of our own godliness. Then life becomes the stuff of holiness for us, not a spiritual threat. Human life becomes the eternal life of the spirit.

⁓

BIBLICAL WISDOM

Do not fear, O soil; be glad and rejoice, for the Lord has done great things! Do not fear, you animals of the field, for the pastures of the wilderness are green; the tree bears its fruit, the fig tree and vine give their full yield. Joel 2:21

SILENCE FOR MEDITATION

QUESTIONS TO PONDER

- In what ways do the painful conditions that confront our planet today—ecological degradation, war, poverty, homelessness—challenge us to rethink our understanding of God and what it means to follow God?
- Do you agree that "It is not necessary to withdraw from the world in order to be holy"? Why or why not?
- How (and where) is God encountered in the *world*? How could encountering God in the *world* help you to become "holy"?

PSALM FRAGMENTS

You cause the grass to grow for the cattle,
and plants for people to use,
to bring forth food from the earth,
and wine to gladden the human heart,
oil to make the face shine,
and bread to strengthen the human heart...
People go out to their work
and to their labor until the evening. Psalm 104:14-15, 23

JOURNAL REFLECTIONS

- Do you consider yourself someone who withdraws from the world to encounter God or someone who engages the world to encounter God? Why?
- What could you do to better integrate your "inward life and [your] immersion in life?"
- Are you able to "see the world through God's eyes"? If so, what does it look like? If not, what do you think is blinding you?

PRAYERS OF HOPE & HEALING

Pray for our religions and spiritual traditions that they, too, will become whole; that they, too, will leave behind the false separation of spirit and matter that harms the holiness of life. Pray that each day you will celebrate the sanctity of creation.

PRAYER FOR TODAY

Gentle Spirit, help me to marry silence and speech, prayer and action in my own heart. Teach me the wisdom of being united, one in one, in the flame of your love.

NOTES

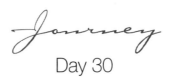

Day 30

SILENCE IS THE ELEMENT OF monastic spirituality that begs for rediscovery in our time. Muzak fills our elevators. Hard rock blares out of cars and boats and apartment house windows. People jog down highways with earphones on and bicycle along city streets balancing boom boxes on their handlebars and sit in airports with transistor radios against their ears, all of them insulated against the world around them and, most of all, protected against the searchings within themselves. Monastic spirituality says we must learn to listen to the cacophony within us in order to defy its demands and to dampen its hold on us.

Monastic spirituality says it is the clamor of the self that needs to be brought to quiet so that the quiet of God can be brought to consciousness. Monastic spirituality says it is the cry of our own passions that mute the cry of others. Monastic spirituality says people comfortable with silence can never live comfortably with noise.

ↄ

BIBLICAL WISDOM

If only you would be altogether silent! For you, that would be wisdom. Job 13:5

SILENCE FOR MEDITATION

QUESTIONS TO PONDER

- We may not all live in monasteries, but we can all develop what Joan Chittister calls "monastic spirituality." How would you describe the values of such a spirituality?
- What place does silence have in the worship experience of your community of faith?
- Why do you suppose our culture encourages constant noise rather than silence?

PSALM FRAGMENTS

For God alone my soul waits in silence,
for my hope is from him. Psalm 62:5

JOURNAL REFLECTIONS

- Contemplate whether or not you are comfortable with silence and solitude.
- Do you bring yourself to silence in order that God can be brought to consciousness? If so, write about how you foster silence in your life. If not, what would you need to do to foster silence in your life? Are you ready to do it?
- In what ways do you "listen to the cacophony" within you? What do you learn by listening to the cacophony? As you "listen" does the noise lessen?

PRAYERS OF HOPE & HEALING

Pray for quiet and stillness. Pray that the world will slow down, become more patient, and welcome silence into its midst. Pray for the healing of strife and discord and the coming of peace.

PRAYER FOR TODAY

Silence, great teacher, fill my soul with your perfume! May you make a home in my heart and lead me to feel the pulsing of creation toward holiness.

NOTES

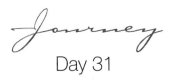

Day 31

LAUGHTER LIBERATES AND LAUGHTER UPLIFTS. When laughter comes into a life, nothing is impossible, nothing is too difficult, nothing can defeat us. We can survive the noonday sun and the darkness of death and the grinding boredom of dailiness and still find life exhilarating. Other things in life change character like chameleons on plaid, but laughter is always ornament, always grace.

Once we learn to laugh and play, we will have come closer to understanding our laughing, playing God. The God of ridiculous promises is a God who laughs, a God to be laughed at and laughed with, until that moment when all pain washes away and only the laughter of God is left to be heard in the heavens.

BIBLICAL WISDOM

Sarah said, "God has brought me laughter, and everyone who hears about this will laugh with me." Genesis 21:6

SILENCE FOR MEDITATION

QUESTIONS TO PONDER

- Does your faith community laugh a lot? What does that tell you?
- How does it make you feel to imagine God as a "laughing, playing God"?
- How might such an image of God change the tone and practice of a community of faith?

PSALM FRAGMENTS

Then our mouth was filled with laughter,
 and our tongue with shouts of joy;
  then it was said among the nations,
"The LORD has done great things for them." Psalm 126:2

Journal Reflections

- Meditate on this question: *Is there enough laughter in my life?*
- In spite of what goes in your life and in the world, do you "find life exhilarating"? If so, is there any relationship between this feeling and how much you laugh? If not, are there ways you could reframe your experience in the light of our "laughing God"?
- Have you experienced God as a "God of ridiculous promises"? If so, how does it make you feel? Like you want to laugh or cry or perhaps be angry? What does that tell you? If not, why not?

Prayers of Hope & Healing

May the goodwill and laughter of the human spirit circle our planet with hope and healing. Pray for the spontaneous joy of God to erupt in your heart and bring laughter to you and to those around you. Pray for the gentle liberation that laughter brings.

Prayer for Today

O, Joyous One! How I long to laugh with you; how I long to wash away all my pain! Your boundless happiness adorns my heart with song.

Notes

Journey

Day 32

PRAYER IS NEITHER A PASSIVE nor an empty act. On the contrary prayer "works." The only problem is that when we pray we get what we seek. What we want out of prayer determines how we go about it. If we want security and protection, we say suffrage prayers; if we want serenity and enlightenment, we meditate; if we want immersion in the mind of Christ, we immerse ourselves in scripture. Prayer is not one kind of activity, it is many. It nourishes the spiritual life; it also reflects it.

When we are young religious, we "say" our prayers. When we get older in the religious life, we "go to prayer." But when we begin to see prayer as the undergirding of life, the pulse of the universe in the center of the soul, we become a prayer. First, as Gandhi says, we have words and no heart; finally, we grow into a heart without words. The *truth* is that the way we pray says something about what we believe about God and about what we believe about life itself. To the monastic mind, prayer is the marking of time and the pursuit of the known but unseen, the fulfilling but unaccomplished. Those qualities mark the prayer life of a monastic community in both form and substance.

⁓

BIBLICAL WISDOM

Therefore I tell you, whatever you ask for in prayer, believe that you have received it, and it will be yours. Mark 11:24

SILENCE FOR MEDITATION

QUESTIONS TO PONDER

- In what ways have you experienced in your faith community that "prayer works"?
- In what ways, if any, does your faith community teach people to "become a prayer"?
- Is praying a "religious" activity or does it transcend religion? Explain.

Psalm Fragments

Therefore let all who are faithful
  offer prayer to you... Psalm 32:6a

Journal Reflections

- Contemplate your prayer life. When do you pray? How often do you pray? How do you pray? What do you pray for?
- Are you happy with your prayer life? If so, what is the ground of your happiness? If not, what changes could you make to your daily routines and practices in order for prayer to become a more central part of your life?
- With respect to prayer, imagine in your journal what it would be like to "grow into a heart without words."

Prayers of Hope & Healing

Send prayers out to all creation, that our belonging to God will become more than an activity in us; it will be the pulse of the universe itself. Pray for the ability to pray without ceasing, to have your life "become a prayer." Pray with your whole heart and whole soul for your loved ones, and for life itself.

Prayer for Today

May my heart expand without words into the silence of your love. Anoint me, Divine One, with the wisdom of the unseen.

Notes

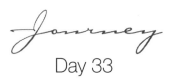

Day 33

ALMOST TWENTY-FIVE HUNDRED YEARS AGO the philosopher Plato wrote one of the most commonly cited dictums in the English language. "The unexamined life," he said, "is not worth living." …Here, clearly is an insight that the world knows to be important. It carries a truth—a challenge—that clings like a tick to the human soul. The longer I live, the more convinced I become of the fundamental truth of it, the more I wonder at the same time how many people really—consciously—rummage the ground, search out the underpinnings of the lives they lead. After all, it's a dangerous process…

The ability—the commitment—to question, to examine every aspect of the human journey is the only form of fidelity worth the price of admission to this sojourn called life. Otherwise, no sector of the social anatomy to which we share allegiance can trust us to serve it well. It is the questions we ask that move us from stage to stage of our growing, that take us from level to level of our thoughts, however simple the questions may seem.

BIBLICAL WISDOM

You said, "Listen now, and I will speak; I will question you, and you shall answer me." Job 42:4

SILENCE FOR MEDITATION

QUESTIONS TO PONDER

- How might Plato's wisdom—"The unexamined life is not worth living"—be of benefit to your spiritual community?
- In what ways does our culture discourage people from truly examining their lives?
- Why is the commitment to question "a form of fidelity"? What does this tell us about God?

PSALM FRAGMENTS

Prove me, O LORD, and try me;
test my heart and mind. Psalm 26:2

JOURNAL REFLECTIONS

- Write down in your journal the areas of your life that need to be questioned and examined.
- In what ways do you presently go about examining your life? What do you need to do to open yourself further to self-examination and growth? Do you have a *truth teller*, someone to help you examine your life? If not, could you find one?
- Meditate on the idea that questioning your life is "a dangerous process." Do you agree? Why or why not?

PRAYERS OF HOPE & HEALING

Pray for our religious and political leaders that they will find the moral strength to examine their lives and work. Pray for the tenacity of heart that never gives up and remains ever faithful to God's gift of truth. Pray for the gift of insight, so your spiritual life will continue to grow in depth.

PRAYER FOR TODAY

Today, and all the days of my life, grant me the strength to examine my heart. May I be faithful, God, to your gift of truth in me.

NOTES

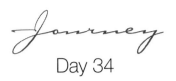

Day 34

WE NOW FACE THE QUESTION of the tension between the catechetical and the mystical, the dogmatic and the spiritual, that is infecting every dimension of modern life. We want rules and dogmas and systems and hierarchies so that we can tell who has the power, who's right and who's wrong, who's on top and who doesn't count at all. That way we can dispose of the earth, the animals, and the women without contest and call all of it God's will.

Until feeling becomes as important as thinking, as important to the spiritual life as rituals and rules, we will continue to have religion but we will never find spirituality, we will have countries but we will never have culture, we will have liturgy but we will never have holiness, we will have religious life but we will never have religious.

Until we concern ourselves with how people feel as a result of what we do, we have not really thought a thing through—at all. Feeling is not non-thinking. Feeling is another way of thinking. Feeling may be the only thing that, in the end, can finally take us beyond the structures and politics and shifting dogmas of the church into the heart of God.

*

BIBLICAL WISDOM

But the Lord was gracious to them and had compassion and showed concern for them because of his covenant with Abraham, Isaac, and Jacob. 2 Kings 13:23

SILENCE FOR MEDITATION

QUESTIONS TO PONDER

- What role, if any, does feeling have in your faith community?
- In what ways do culture and religion oppress feelings?
- Do you agree that "feeling may be the only thing that…can finally take us into the heart of God"? Explore your response.

Psalm Fragments

I keep the LORD always before me;
because he is at my right hand, I shall not be moved.
Therefore my heart is glad, and my soul rejoices;
my body also rests secure. Psalm 16:8-9

Journal Reflections

- In your life of faith, are you primarily committed to the "catechetical" or the mystical," the "dogmatic" or the "spiritual"? Explain.
- In your life, is feeling "as important as thinking"? If so, what does that mean for you? If not, what role does feeling play in your life?
- Reflect on experiences where your feelings have moved you to act on behalf of others. Reflect on experiences when the feelings of others have changed the way you act.

Prayers of Hope & Healing

Pray for your family and spiritual community that true feeling will be expressed and hope will be restored. Pray that the citizens of our planet will feel the suffering plight of others and open their hearts to God's wish. Pray for the ability to be passionate and committed, to experience the Spirit's longing in you.

Prayer for Today

May my heart groan with those who are pained and feel anguish with those who suffer oppression. May my soul feel your pathos, God, for our world.

Notes

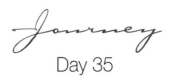

Day 35

MOHANDAS GANDHI WROTE, "I HAVE only three enemies. My favorite enemy, the one most easily influenced for the better, is the British nation. My second enemy, the Indian people, is far more difficult. But my most formidable opponent is a man named Mohandas K. Gandhi. With him I seem to have very little influence…"

His third enemy, himself, was his only clear victory. He had immersed himself totally in God… He had raised *ahimsa*, nonviolence, to the level of the political. He made religious discipline—meditation, fasting, self-control—the raw material of limitless strength. He turned himself and all his weaknesses into a channel of light for others. He became totally pure of heart, the one in whom there is no guile, the *mahatma*, the "great soul" who, loving all the others, lived for them and so became holy himself.

BIBLICAL WISDOM

In your unfailing love you will lead the people you have redeemed. In your strength you will guide them to your holy dwelling. Exodus 15:13

SILENCE FOR MEDITATION

QUESTIONS TO PONDER

- Do you think that *ahimsa*, nonviolence, should be the basis for Christian religious communities? Why or why not?
- If *ahimsa* were the basis of Christian communities of faith, how might the interpretation of Scripture, the practice of worship, and engagement in social justice change?
- Do Gandhi's religious disciplines—meditation, fasting, self-control—make sense for ordinary Christians today? If so, how can they be fostered? If not, why not?

Psalm Fragments

As for what others do, by the word of your lips
I have avoided the ways of the violent.
My steps have held fast to your paths;
my feet have not slipped. Psalm 17:4-5

Journal Reflections

- Who is your "favorite enemy," your "most formidable opponent"? How do you confront this enemy?
- Make a list of the spiritual leaders (living or dead) whom you admire. What are their attributes and activities that you would like to integrate into your own spiritual life? How would you begin doing it?
- Have you ever practiced meditation and fasting as spiritual disciplines? If so, write about the experience and its impact on your spiritual life. If not, can you imagine learning and practicing these disciplines?

Prayers of Hope & Healing

Pray for nonviolence of thought, word, and deed. Pray for a heart filled with concern for others. Pray that the great souls, saints, and martyrs of history will illuminate our lives and lead us to greater holiness.

Prayer for Today

Blessed are you, Creator, for the many souls of light that have illuminated my path. May their memory and the memory of all your saints shine with compassion on our world.

Notes

Day 36

RUMI WAS A SUFI, PART of the mystical tradition of Islam that calls the Muslim community to be especially conscious of the teachings of the Koran on the transitoriness of life in this world. In its earliest form, Sufism was deeply and rigorously ascetic... From its emphasis on spiritual austerity, however, Sufism gradually turned more to concern for the love of God than for the wrath of God. Sufism shifted its concentration from asceticism to mysticism... Sufism was not looking for rewards in the next life; Sufism was looking for union with God in this one...

Rumi left the world a body of poetry that made the human condition a holy one and a corpus of religious wisdom in common language that far surpassed the understandings and teachings of the structures and institutions of the time. Rumi's poetry dealt with the divine nature of life, the meaning of human love, and the reality of union with God. Rumi touched the world with a wand of goodness.

ɔ

BIBLICAL WISDOM

My purpose is that they may be encouraged in heart and united in love, so that they may have the full riches of complete understanding, in order that they may know the mystery of God. Colossians 2:2

SILENCE FOR MEDITATION

QUESTIONS TO PONDER

- Joan Chittister suggests that there is much to learn from other religious traditions such as Sufism. Do you agree? Why or why not?
- In what ways, if any, does your community of faith facilitate learning about other religions and engaging with the adherents of other religions? Could more be done?
- In what way does Sufism's quest for "union with God" in this life find expression in your own religion or spiritual tradition?

PSALM FRAGMENTS

But you, O Lord, are a God merciful and gracious,
slow to anger and abounding in steadfast love and faithfulness. Psalm 86:15

JOURNAL REFLECTIONS

- A central tenet of Sufism is that God's mercy is greater than God's wrath. Meditate on both God's mercy and wrath. In your own life of faith, do you find yourself dwelling more on the mercy of God or on the wrath of God? Why?
- Do you find yourself longing for mystical understanding and experience? If so, what are you doing to answer your longing? If not, why not?
- In your journal, write about how you understand the "divine nature of life, the meaning of human love, and the reality of union with God."

PRAYERS OF HOPE & HEALING

May Rumi's passion for God overflow our hearts and overcome our timidity. May his experience of union with God become a beacon of hope for us and for our communities. Let us pray for the deep desire of love to fill us with longing, until our hearts and God's heart are one.

PRAYER FOR TODAY

As you have bestowed mercy on me, O God, may my heart grow in love and forgiveness for my own and others' sins. Lead me to your inner sanctum, to the white light of union.

NOTES

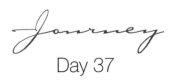

Day 37

FOR NO ACCEPTABLE REASON, LOSS destabilizes even the most sophisticated of us, spilling us off the carousel of commonplaces we thought would never end. With little warning, with less compensation, we find ourselves left to cope with an abandoned pattern of happy yesterdays left spinning in a blur of bleak tomorrows...

To be left without the mainstay of a life is to be plunged into questioning the rest of it. To what end is life without this position, this support, this thing, this person? To what purpose is a future that has no living past? The tomorrow that, once a given, now has no design? The hope that has gone to dust, the prospect turned to mist? What can possibly be left to live for, even though, for whatever reason, live we must? Where is the will of God for us in loss?

⌐

BIBLICAL WISDOM

Blessed are those who mourn, for they will be comforted. Matthew 5:4

SILENCE FOR MEDITATION

QUESTIONS TO PONDER

- In practical terms, how does your community of faith help people to live through the experience of loss and grief? Is there more that could be done?
- If the questioning that accompanies loss were seen as a process of spiritual development, what kind of assistance should be given to people suffering loss?
- Where is the "will of God" in the experience of loss?

Psalm Fragments

Be merciful to me, O Lord, for I am in distress;
my eyes grow weak with sorrow,
my soul and my body with grief. Psalm 31:9

Journal Reflections

- Meditate on your experiences of great loss. As a result of these losses, did you experience the destabilization of your life? Describe the experience.
- Where was God in the losses you have experienced, either in the past or in the present?
- Have you ever thought, in the wake of great loss: "What can possibly be left to live for, even though, for whatever reason, live [I] must"? What answers emerged for you during the grief process?

Prayers of Hope & Healing

Pray that God will be present in the midst of loss and questioning. Pray for the wisdom to experience life's changes with compassion and peace. Pray that love will overcome sorrow and hope will overcome despair.

Prayer for Today

Show me, Fount of Mercy, where I can find you! Come to me, Merciful One, and be a rudder for my wandering soul.

Notes

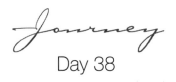

Day 38

"THE RULE OF FRIENDSHIP," THE Buddha said, "means there should be mutual sympathy between them, each supplying what the other lacks and trying to benefit the other…" The words ring true. Friendship is not as much a matter of happenstance as we are inclined to think.

Perhaps one of life's most precious lessons is that we must learn to choose our friends as well as to find them. The corollary of the insight, of course, is that we must learn not to allow ourselves simply to fall into alliances and acquaintanceships that come and go like starlight on the water, exciting for a while but easily forgotten. We must learn, in other words, not to make life a playground of faceless, nameless people—all of whom are useful for awhile but who never really touch the soul or stretch the mind or prod the conscience.

BIBLICAL WISDOM

Jonathan said to David, "Go in peace, for we have sworn friendship with each other in the name of the Lord, saying, 'The Lord is witness between you and me, and between your descendants and my descendants forever.'" Isaiah 20:42

SILENCE FOR MEDITATION

QUESTIONS TO PONDER

- How has contemporary culture affected the capacity (positively or negatively) to achieve deep friendships?
- What is the true value of friendship?
- Describe the relationship and/or difference between "finding" friends and "choosing" friends.

Psalm Fragments

Pray for the peace of Jerusalem:
> *"May they prosper who love you.*
Peace be within your walls,
> *and security within your towers."*
For the sake of my relatives and friends
> *I will say, "Peace be within you."* Psalm 122:6-8

Journal Reflections

- How would you describe your own "rule of friendship"? Does Buddha's definition have meaning for you? Why or why not? What criteria do you use when choosing friends?
- Make a list of your closest friends. Describe how either the Buddha's rule of friendship or your own rule of friendship works in those relationships.
- Meditate on how your friendships mutually "really touch the soul or stretch the mind or prod the conscience."

Prayers of Hope & Healing

Pray for your community of friends that God will sustain and nourish their souls and lead them to greater understanding and wisdom. Pray for all those who are without true friends that God will anoint them with love. May our friendships be honored and respected as we continue to grow in the Spirit.

Prayer for Today

Thank you, Great Mystery, for all the friends in my life. Thank you for their love and honesty. May I become a more committed and generous friend in all my relations.

Notes

Day 39

To GROW AS A PERSON there is one question that is fundamental: "For what purpose might this decision of mine be wrong?" Because I have not pursued all the facts? Because I have not asked the right questions? Because I have not consulted others in the process of forming it? Because I refuse to even think of adjusting to another way of doing things? Because I am too arrogant to even ask the questions?

Questions are not simply instruments of social change. They are also agents of social bonding. Sometimes, instead of asking questions of another person, in our panic we talk only about ourselves and then wonder why the person does not respond. Gertrude Stein tells us how to solve the quandary of what question to ask to open a conversation: "How do you like what you have? This is a question that anybody can ask of anybody. Ask it." And then watch your social life flower.

BIBLICAL WISDOM

When the queen of Sheba heard of Solomon's fame, she came to Jerusalem to test him with hard questions. Arriving with a very great caravan—with camels carry-ing spices, large quantities of gold, and precious stones—she came to Solomon and talked with him about all she had on her mind. 2 Chronicles 9:1

SILENCE FOR MEDITATION

QUESTIONS TO PONDER

- In what ways might questions be "agents of social bonding"?
- How would your religious community change if questions were seen as "agents of social bonding" rather than challenges to existing rituals, rules, or privilege?
- What are the big or taboo questions for your religion or family today? How do you deal with these questions? What might you do to make them occasions of transformation rather than fear?

Psalm Fragments

I say to the Lord, "You are my Lord;
I have no good apart from you." Psalm 16:2

Journal Reflections

- Meditate on your own deep questions? Do you allow yourself truly to listen to them and to seek answers? Where do you go to seek answers? Are there other places (or people) where you could seek answers?
- Contemplate Gertrude Stein's question: "How do you like what you have?" and then write down your response. Sometime today ask this question of a friend and just listen.
- Do you consider yourself to be a good listener? Why or why not?

Prayers of Hope & Healing

Pray for the fidelity to ask true questions and to be free from arrogance, resistance, or fear. Pray for the humility to hear others express their needs and to listen to their heart's longing. Pray that the freedom of truth-seeking will be the measure of the Spirit's indwelling in us.

Prayer for Today

Thank you for the freedom to question. Thank you for the joy of not-knowing. Make my heart humble before your glory.

Notes

Day 40

WE SO OFTEN THINK THAT those who refuse under any conditions to deny the essential goodness of life are mad. Look at suffering. Look at evil. Be real, we say. We are so often inclined to think that those who continue to see life where life seems to be empty and futile are, at best, foolish. Be sensible, we say. But in that case, we may be the ones who are mad. The truth is that contemplation, the ability to see behind the obvious to the soul of life, is the ultimate sanity. The contemplative sees life as it really is under all the struggle and the pain: imbued with God, glowing with eternity, full of energy, and so overflowing with good that evil never totally triumphs.

Contemplation keeps the inner eye focused on Goodness… Contemplation is not a spiritual fad or some kind of religious trick… Contemplation is the crown of the spirit, the gateway of the heart through which all good comes and in which all things are welcome as gifts of God. Contemplation exists across time, across traditions, beyond cultures, outside of creeds, despite denominational cautions or priestly prescriptions to the contrary. Awareness of the presence of God in the stuff of the daily, the everywhere, the always, the everyone, undergirds every major spiritual path… It is not the contemplative who is mad. It is the rest of the world who lack what it takes to be sane in an often insane world.

෴

BIBLICAL WISDOM

And the Lord said, "I will cause all my goodness to pass in front of you, and I will proclaim my name, the Lord, in your presence. I will have mercy on whom I will have mercy, and I will have compassion on whom I will have compassion." Exodus 33:19

SILENCE FOR MEDITATION

QUESTIONS TO PONDER

- If your community of faith kept their "inner eye focused on Goodness", how would your experience of spirituality be different? What would your heart feel?

- Do you agree: "It is not the contemplative who is mad"? Why or why not?
- If you are a contemplative, how has contemplation allowed you to see beneath the surface of things to the "ultimate sanity of life"? If you are not a contemplative, can you imagine taking up the practice? How would you get started?

PSALM FRAGMENTS

The heavens are telling the glory of God;
and the firmament proclaims his handiwork.
Day to day pours forth speech,
and night to night declares knowledge.
There is no speech, nor are there words;
their voice is not heard;
yet their voice goes out through all the earth,
and their words to the end of the world. Psalm 19:1-4

JOURNAL REFLECTIONS

- One of the most important needs for spiritual development is to know your own goodness. Write about how you understand your inner goodness.
- In your journal, consider the challenges and opportunities that prevent or encourage your ability to affirm your goodness and the goodness of creation.
- Contemplate the "sanity" of seeing goodness beneath the pain and suffering of life.

PRAYERS OF HOPE & HEALING

Pray for goodness to reign on earth. Pray for the determination to follow your heart's call to beauty and your soul's desire for goodness. Pray that contemplation becomes the guiding light of humanity and its future.

PRAYER FOR TODAY

Blessed be You, who bestows all Goodness. Blessed be You, heart of hearts. Blessed be You, who contemplates life through creation.

NOTES

Journey's End

You have finished your *40-Day Journey with Joan Chittister*. I hope it has been a good journey and that along the way you have learned much and experienced much and found good resources to deepen your faith and practice. As a result of this journey:

- How are you different?
- What have you learned?
- What have you experienced?
- In what ways has your faith and practice been transformed?

Notes

Do you want to continue the journey? If you would, there is a list of Sister Joan's books on the next page that will help you delve further into the thought, experience, and practice of this remarkable woman.

FOR FURTHER READING

A Passion for Life: Fragments of the Face of God. Maryknoll: Orbis, 2001.

Becoming Fully Human: The Greatest Glory of God. New York: Sheed & Ward, 2005.

Beyond Beijing: The Next Step for Women. New York: Sheed & Ward, 1996.

Called to Question: A Spiritual Memoir. New York: Sheed & Ward, 2004.

Heart of Flesh: A Feminist Spirituality for Women and Men. Grand Rapids: Eerdmans, 1998.

Illuminated Life: Monastic Wisdom for Seekers of Light. Maryknoll: Orbis, 2005.

In Search of Belief. Liguori: Liguori, 1999, 2006.

In the Heart of the Temple: My Spiritual Vision for Today's World. New York: BlueBridge, 2004.

Scarred by Struggle, Transformed by Hope. Grand Rapids: Eerdmans, 2003.

Seeing with Our Souls: Monastic Wisdom for Every Day. New York: Sheed & Ward, 2002.

The Friendship of Women: The Hidden Tradition of the Bible. New York: Blue-Bridge, 2006.

The Story of Ruth: Twelve Moments in Every Woman's Life. Grand Rapids: Eerdmans, 2000.

The Tent of Abraham: Stories of Hope and Peace for Jews, Christians, and Muslims. Boston: Beacon, 2006.

"The Power of Questions to Propel: A Retrospective," in *Spiritual Questions for the Twenty-First Century,* ed. Mary Hembrow Snyder. Maryknoll: Orbis, 2001.

The Way We Were: A Story of Conversion and Renewal. Maryknoll: Orbis, 2005.

There Is a Season. Maryknoll: Orbis, 1995.

Wisdom Distilled from the Daily: Living the Rule of St. Benedict Today. San Francisco: HarperSanFrancisco, 1990.

Women, Ministry, and the Church. New York: Paulist, 1983.

Visit Sister Joan at her website: www.Benetvision.org.

NOTES

All of the following citations are from works by Joan Chittister
Page 9, paragraph 3: www.msnbc.com/id/12283802/
Page 9, paragraph 4: www.beliefnet.com/blogs/godspolitics/2007/05/voice
-of-day-joan-chittister_25.html
Page 10, paragraph 1: *Songs of Joy: New Meditations on the Psalms for Every
Day of the Year* (New York: Crossroad), 10.
Page 10, paragraph 3: burkelecture.ucsd.edu/past/chittister.html
Page 10, paragraph 4: *Songs of Joy: New Meditations on the Psalms for Every
Day of the Year* (New York: Crossroad), 97.

Sources

Day 1: *Called to Question,* 19

Day 2: *Becoming Fully Human,* 96

Day 3: *Called to Question,* 22

Day 4: *Wisdom Distilled from the Daily,* 43

Day 5: *In the Heart of the Temple,* 33

Day 6: *Heart of Flesh,* 50

Day 7: *In the Heart of the Temple,* 55

Day 8: *Becoming Fully Human,* 107-8

Day 9: *Beyond Beijing,* 157-58

Day 10: *Illuminated Life,* 15, 19

Day 11: *Illuminated Life,* 36-37

Day 12: *Illuminated Life,* 94

Day 13: *Scarred by Struggle,* 80

Day 14: *Scarred by Struggle,* 66-67

Day 15: *There Is a Season,* 20-21

Day 16: *There Is a Season,* 90

Day 17: *There Is a Season,* 108

Day 18: *Called to Question*, 166-67

Day 19: *Heart of Flesh*, 89-90

Day 20: *Women, Ministry, and the Church*, 7-8

Day 21: *Wisdom Distilled from the Daily*, 64-65

Day 22: *Wisdom Distilled from the Daily*, 130-31

Day 23: *The Way We Were*, 49

Day 24: *In Search of Belief*, 43

Day 25: *Beyond Beijing*, 152-53

Day 26: *The Tent of Abraham*, 92-93

Day 27: *Becoming Fully Human*, 98, 99

Day 28: *Wisdom Distilled from the Daily*, 168

Day 29: *Called to Question*, 101

Day 30: *Wisdom Distilled from the Daily*, 169

Day 31: *There Is a Season*, 36, 39

Day 32: *In the Heart of the Temple*, 38

Day 33: *The Power of Questions to Propel*, 167-68

Day 34: *The Power of Questions to Propel*, 185-86

Day 35: *A Passion for Life*, 5, 8

Day 36: *A Passion for Life*, 27-28

Day 37: *The Story of Ruth*, 10-11

Day 38: *The Friendship of Women*, 15-16

Day 39: *Seeing with Our Souls*, 81

Day 40: *Illuminated Life*, 140-41

We gratefully acknowledge the publishers who granted permission to reprint material from the following sources:

Becoming Fully Human by Joan D. Chittister (Lanham, MD: Sheed & Ward, 2005). Reprinted by permission.

Beyond Beijing: The Next Step for Women by Joan D. Chittister (Lanham, MD: Sheed & Ward, 1996). Reprinted by permission.

Called to Question: A Spiritual Memoir by John D. Chittister, (Lanham, MD: Sheed & Ward, 2004)

The Friendship Of Women by Joan Chittister. Reprinted with permission of United Tribes Media Inc./Blue Bridge.

Heart of Flesh: A Feminist Spirituality for Women and Men by Joan Chittister. © 1998 Wm B. Eerdmans Publishing Company. All rights reserved. Used with permission of the publisher and Novalis, Saint Paul University, Ottawa.

Illuminated Life by Joan Chittister, © 2000 Joan Chittister (Maryknoll, New York: Orbis). Reprinted by permission.

In Search of Belief copyright ©1999, 2006. Used with permission of Liguori Publications, Liguori, MO 63057. 1-800-325-9521.www.liguori.org

In the Heart of the Temple: My Spiritual Vision for Today's World by Joan Chittister. Reprinted with permission of United Tribes Media Inc./Blue Bridge.

A Passion for Life: Fragments of the Face of God by Joan Chittister, © 1996 Joan Chittister, OSB (Maryknoll: Orbis). Reprinted by permission.

Scarred by Struggle, Transformed by Hope, by Joan D. Chittister. © 2005 Wm B. Eerdmans Publishing Company. All rights reserved. Used with permission of the publisher and Novalis, Saint Paul University, Ottawa.

Seeing with Our Souls by Joan D. Chittister (Lanham, MD: Sheed & Ward, 2002). Reprinted by permission.

From "The Power of Question to Propel: A Retrospective," Afterword in *Spiritual Questions for the Twenty-First Century: Essays in Honor of Joan D. Chittister* edited by Mary Hembrow Snyder. Maryknoll: Orbis, 2001. Reprinted by permission.

The Story of Ruth, Twelve Moments in Every Woman's Life, by Joan D. Chittister. © 2000 Wm B. Eerdmans Publishing Company. All rights reserved. Used with permission of the publisher and Novalis, Saint Paul University, Ottawa.

Tent of Abraham by Joan Chittister, Murshid Saadi Shakur Chishti, and Rabbi Arthus Waskow. Copyright © 2006 by Benetvision, Neil Douglas-Klotz, and Arthur Waskow. Reprinted by permission of Beacon Press, Boston.

There Is a Season by Joan Chittister, © 1995 Joan Chittister (Maryknoll: Orbis, 1995). Reprinted by permission.

The Way We Were: A Story of Conversion and Renewal by Joan Chittister, © 2005 Joan Chittister. (Maryknoll: Orbis). Reprinted by permission.

Wisdom Distilled from the Daily: Living the Rule of St. Benedict Today by Joan Chittister. Copyright © 1990 by Joan D. Chittister. Reprinted by permission of HarperCollins Publishers

Women, Ministry and the Church, by Joan Chittister, Copyright © 1983, Paulist Press, Inc., New York/Mahway, NJ. Used with permission of Paulist Press. www.paulistpress.com

NOTES

NOTES

NOTES